To my Attorney
Mr. Dave [illegible]
Author
[illegible]

The Law and Three Shattered Dreams

by

Obie Nickels

VANTAGE PRESS
New York / Washington / Atlanta
Los Angeles / Chicago

The stories you are about to read never happened. The book is based upon pure imagination.

FIRST EDITION

Published by Vantage Press, Inc.
516 West 34th Street, New York, New York 10001

Manufactured in the United States of America
Standard Book Number 533-03910-X

Library of Congress Catalog Card No.: 78-69830

Contents

Introduction

This book will cover the lives of three people who had a dream. They all had a dream of becoming just a little more successful in life than they already were. But what these three people didn't realize was, the law plays a major part in all aspects of gaining success. Sometimes it's on your side, and other times it plays the odds against you. Like in Fred Jones's story, "The Warden's Daughter." Fred Jones, using the name Frank Jackson, almost spent the rest of his life in prison. If it hadn't been for the law working in his behalf, he would have. He had fallen and his dream was already shattered, but the law took a different turn and went to his side. That's why he looks back and says, "It never would have happened if it hadn't been for the warden's daughter."

Tommie Foley wasn't so lucky. He wasn't asking for that much out of his dream. He only wanted to be the first black foreman on his job. He knew he could handle the job, so did everybody else. And they all knew he deserved to be given a chance. And he was just about to be given that chance when the law came along and shattered his dream. Tommie looks back and says, "Not only was my dream shattered, my whole life was shattered." And he calls it, "My Last Christmas."

Leo Servettie, one time bank robber and a loser, sat out fifteen years in prison dreaming up a way to beat the law, and twice he did. And as he had planned it, the law was going 'round and 'round in circles, playing the old tune, "Who Did It?" But Leo made one little mistake in the second robbery that gave the F.B.I. just enough of a peephole to put an end to Leo's dream and bring a close to the "Small Town Robberies."

THE LAW
AND THREE SHATTERED DREAMS

The Warden's Daughter

When you're serving time in prison, strange things happen to you. Not only the guys you're living with will shoot you off in a double cross, but the guys that turn the keys on you will also double-cross you—and, boy, speaking of a double cross, I sure as hell got put in a big one—and out of all the people to be doubled-crossed by, it had to be the warden's daughter.

My name is Fred Jones, but when I first went into the Giant I was Frank Jackson, so everybody there all gave me the nickname "Frankie." So for now, let's say I am Frankie.

Although I am out now, the thought of how it came about and how the ordeal went forces me to tell the story.

Well, looking back, things started on the downfall for me just a little ways back—that was before I came in contact with the Giant. You see, in the past I was a private investigator, and my luck didn't go so good at that. It started happening when one of my clients ended up at the bottom of the Gila River and the money he had just drawn out of the Great National Bank in Casa Grande, Arizona, ended up in my apartment, with me out cold and the briefcase handcuffed to my wrist.

I couldn't convince the King and his twelve knights that I wasn't their man, so they sent me down to the state prison to do an eight-to-ten stretch. They knew I didn't ice the guy, but they felt I had a part in it—that's why I got off so light.

After I had spent seven years, six months, and fourteen days there, the judge sent the warden and me a letter telling us that the law had finally broken the case, and that they now had the right man. But instead of taking it on the chin and admitting they made a mistake, they decided to send me home in thirty days. So inside of that thirty days is when all hell broke loose. The gang-detail I was working on had just finished unloading some logs outside the warden's house. The work hadn't been too hard. Sergeant Moorehouse, who was running the detail, told Benny to take the truck back up to the motor pool. He said, "Now the rest of you guys head on back up to the front gate. I'll meet you there." The warden was driving up just as we was leaving. I was back at the end of the line.

The warden got out of his car, took a few steps and stopped. The warden was a lean, tight-lipped, little man, well into his middle years. He was perhaps fifty, or even older, and his reddish hair was shot with a tinge of smokey gray which accentuated the dark leathery quality of his face. A lifetime out of doors in the Arizona sun and winds had stamped him with its own peculiar seal. He called me.

He said, "Hey, Frankie."

I stopped and turned around.

He said, "I understand you will be leaving us soon."

I said, "Yes, sir."

He said, "Well, I just wanted to wish you luck."

I said, "Thank you, sir."

He started to walk off.

I said, "Oh, warden, just thought I would let you know those logs are not stuck too good. They could easily start rolling. You might keep the kids off them."

He didn't say anything.

I said, "Well, just thought I would let you know."

I turned and started walking away.

He said, "How would you like to come up tomorrow and fix them so they won't roll?"

I said, "I don't mind it at all, so long as it's OK with Captain Bennett, and I can get out the gate."

He said, "Don't worry, I'll fix that."

I said, "Well, in that case, I'll see you tomorrow."

When I finally made it to the gate where the rest of the guys were, they all started giving me the old one-two for getting the job at the warden's house.

Danny said, "Hey, you fellows, don't knock it because Frankie slipped the grease to the old boy. Hell, he wasn't thinking about the logs, he was just trying to get close enough to the warden's daughter to make a date for Saturday night."

They all started laughing.

The tower guard heard all the noise. He said, "OK, you fellows, let's cut the chatter and come in when your name is called." Everybody got quiet. You didn't give those guys with the guns any back-talk, because they made the difference, whether you stayed or left those walls.

Finally all our numbers were called, and we all headed back to the cellblock. We knew we would only have time to wash up and go to chow, return to the cellblock, and listen to Leo string out some bad blues. Leo was my cell partner. Every evening before the light went out, Leo would sing and play the blues for the whole cellblock. Even the guards would pitch an ear or two toward that. So that evening, after we all had finished chow and the count was cleared, Leo started fingering away on his guitar. I, for one, could always tell when Leo felt low and was in one of his blue moods. He would just come back to the cellblock and sit down right by the cell door.

You see, Leo didn't talk much. He didn't even receive any mail from home. He had been my cell partner ever since I had been there. And before I got there, he never did have a cell partner.

Once I asked him why he didn't receive any mail, and did he have anybody on the outside?

He said, "What people? I don't have any. The ones I had, I didn't see them in over fifteen years before I came to this Giant. And you know how the old story goes about friends. You got them so long as you don't need them."

So here Leo was again, right back in one of his blue moods, and getting ready to talk to everybody in the cell block the only way he knew to get everybody's attention. And he knew they would all get the message; somehow.

Snowflakes called down from the upper tier. He said, "Hey, Leo, how about something way down, man? You know, like putting a guy in the alley, I want you to lay me down low tonight."

Leo studied for a moment, then he said, "I know where to reach you, man. You got it. You get the speaker plugged in up there and tell all the rest of those cats that old Leo is on the air, and I am going to put it down hard and heavy tonight."

There was another speaker downstairs, so I dropped the cord down to Lieutenant Foley and asked him to plug it into the speaker for me. I took the mike and blew through it.

Then I said, "You guys, stand by, old Leo is on the air. And what he's going to tell you tonight will make you bend those steel bars in front of you."

I walked over to my bunk and sat down on the side. Leo got his guitar and just sat right down at the cell door, crossed his legs and started hammering out "Those Lonesome Jailhouse Blues." Now you have to be locked up and hear Leo sing those kind of blues before you can attempt to understand them and get any idea why the lyrics rhyme like they do. It's like someone sitting down talking to you.

I stood up and took a look around the cellblock. Man, those cats had dropped those pens and pencils. Some were just sitting there with heads down . . . others had just walked up to the cell doors to lean on the bars. Some were just standing there holding on to the bars, tears dropping from their cheeks.

I took a look down at the guards, and they, too, were taking it all in. The way those guards were looking, you would have thought they were the ones locked up. But that's the way it was when Leo really got down. Everybody in the cellblock listened, even the guards.

So that's the way the lights went out that night, with Leo playing the blues. You might say that's the way Leo put us to bed and sent the guards home, at least three times a week.

The next morning I heard my number (24357) called over the P.A. system. They wanted me to report to the yard office.

I looked at Leo and said, "So long, blues man, see you tonight."

He said, "Right on, man."

I heard the guard who was turning the keys say, "24357, and 24357 only, step out when your door is open." I did like I was told.

When I reached the yard office, the guard stopped me out front. He said, "Wait here. The captain wants to see you." A few minutes later he came back. He unlocked the door and said, "This way, and take your hat off." I took my hat off. He pointed to Captain Bennett's office.

Once inside Captain Bennett's office, he never looked up. He said, "What about this, you're supposed to go to the warden's house? What's the matter, don't he have enough people outside to do his errand-running and work?"

I still didn't say anything.

He slowly lifted his head up and said, "What's the matter, don't you hear me talking to you, boy?"

I said, "Why didn't you ask the warden? He was the one who asked me to do the work."

Captain Bennett didn't like that too well. He got to his feet; his face was hard as nails. He leaned across the desk.

He said, "Now you look here, don't you go getting smart with me, goddammit. I don't like this idea one bit. Now you get the hell out of here until I find out what this is all about. On the other hand [he pointed to the guard], have him wait outside the yard office. I am going to find out what this is all about. Somebody is going to tell me what's going on."

The guard looked at me and said, "OK, you, outside."

The captain was dialing the warden's number as I was leaving. I was behind the guard, so I didn't close the door. When he went down to tell the other guard that I would be waiting out in the hall, I took my toe and pushed the captain's door open just enough to hear the conversation.

When the warden answered the phone, Captain Bennett said, "Warden, this is Bennett. What is this about Frankie working up at your house? I know, sir, that he is going home in thirty days, but he is still no trustee outside yet. I thought maybe if you had one of the men out—but, sir—but, sir, I don't—yes, sir. But, sir. Yes, sir. I know, sir—yes, sir. Right away, sir."

I knew the warden was giving him hell for questioning his decision.

Captain Bennett yelled to the guard, "Get that man back here."

I slowly walked back into the office and said, "Did you find out whether I go outside or stay, sir?"

Boy he was mad as hell. He said, "Mr. Miles, get this man out to the front gate. Lieutenant Bassey will pick him up there."

He looked at me and said, "Now get the hell out of here."

I said, "I thank the captain, and don't worry, I'll be back."

He looked at the guard and said, "Mr. Miles, will you get this man the hell out of here—and you, too."

The guard and I headed out to the front gate. On my way there, a thought came to me. Lieutenant Rim Bassey, old Big Rim, that's what everybody called him, from what I had heard didn't like convicts working around the warden's house. He had sent everybody back to the walls that had worked at the warden's house. And to my count, he had sent back eight so far. I didn't let the thought bother me because I was already living inside the walls. But I knew I was the first to go from the walls and work for the warden. I let the thought pass, being that I was only going to be out there for one day.

The guard and I reached the gates, and sure enough Big Rim was waiting. He looked up at the tower guard and said, "I'll take this number 24357 with me. Open the gate, Al, and let him out."

When the gates opened I walked out. Big Rim took a long look at me. Then he said, "So you are the one that's supposed to go to work for the warden?"

I said, "Yes, but I wish I wasn't."

He said, "So do I. But since you are, just let me give you a piece of advice. You're going up there to work, so that's what I want to see you doing every time I make checks. And another thing, I'll be watching you every minute. Now get on the back of that pickup and let's go."

I jumped on back of the truck, like he said. He got in and headed out to the warden's house. I began to hate myself for mentioning those Goddamn logs to the warden. I had had nothing but hell ever since. First from Captain Bennett, and then from Big Rim. Who knows what kind of hell I would get from the warden.

I knew I couldn't afford to talk back, being that I only had thirty more days to do. So I said to myself, *to hell with it, I am not going to let a day's work blow my chance of getting the hell out of this hell hole.* I had been waiting to go home for eight long years.

When we reached the warden's house, Big Rim said, "Get down and wait here. I'll get you something to work with."

Just about that time the warden came out of the house. He said, "Good morning. Are you ready to go to work?"

I said, "Yes, sir."

Big Rim said, "I am getting him something to work with now, warden."

Warden Bolden said, "That's all right, Lieutenant Bassey, you can run along, I'll take care of it."

Big Rim wasn't too happy with that. He got in the pickup truck, and for the next few yards, the tires caught hell.

About that time the warden turned to me and said, "Come on, go with me, Frankie, the tool shed is this way. I am sure you will find everything you need to work with. And if there's anything else you need, other than what's in the shed, call my daughter and have her call me at the office. I'll see that you get it at the motorpool."

I said, "Yes, sir."

I looked inside the tool shed and took out the hatchet and sledgehammer. The warden was standing near the log pile. I walked over to where the logs were. I took my foot and kicked the bottom one. They all started rolling. I looked around and there was Big Rim coming out from behind the hedges. He told the warden that he was just passing by and heard all this noise. The warden gave him a dirty look and walked over and got in his car and drove off.

Big Rim walked over to me and said, "You just remember what I said earlier, I'll be watching you every minute."

I said, "You've already proved that," and turned and walked away.

The logs weren't heavy, so moving them wasn't any big problem. I started trimming some stakes to hold the logs in a stack. I had worked about an hour and the hot sun had just about dried me out. I looked around for a water outlet. There wasn't any, so I just kept on working. I didn't want to be caught rambling around the warden's house. I told myself that I only had about another half hour to work, and then I could get all the water I wanted.

I worked with my back to the house. Suddenly I heard a soft voice, almost like a whisper.

"Good morning."

I looked around to see the warden's daughter standing there. And boy was she looking good.

She said, "Pardon me, would you like to have some water? You've been working out here in the hot sun all morning. You must be pretty thirsty."

I lied and said that I wasn't thirsty. I said, "I am only going to be another half hour. Thanks anyway." I turned and started back to work. She never said another word. I looked back and she was headed toward the house. She went in and closed the door.

I was just about to move to the other side when she walked right up behind me.

She said, "Here, I brought you some water. I fixed it with plenty of ice. You looked like you could use it. My daddy told me to make you some. Sorry I took so long, I overslept." She smiled and said, "Daddy also said you mentioned to him about the logs. I am glad. That little brother of mine wouldn't have stopped until he was on top of them." Then she set the bucket down and said, "I'll leave the water here for you. You can have a drink whenever you want it."

I said, "Thanks."

She smiled and turned and walked away.

Once I heard the door close, I stopped working and made a beeline to the water bucket. I started gobbling the water down like crazy. Then all of a sudden I was knocked off my feet with a blow to the stomach. I crawled up on my knees and opened my eyes and discovered Big Rim standing over me. I moved just in time to miss the butt of his rifle, which was aimed at my head.

Then I heard Emily yelling, "Stop it. What are you beating up on him for?" She was running out to where we were. She said, "What is this all about?"

Big Rim said, "This don't concern you."

She said, "The heck it don't. Anytime you come around our house beating up on people for nothing, I want to know why."

Big Rim said, "You have no business butting in. I didn't tell this guy he could have any water breaks."

She said, "For your information, daddy told me to fix Frankie some ice water. And you can believe me, he is going to hear about this. And right now I'd just as soon you leave."

I said, "That's all right, Miss Emily, I'll be through in a few minutes and on my way."

I got up holding my stomach and walked over to the log pile.

Big Rim turned to me and said, "As for you, you just shut up and get to work."

Emily said, "I asked you to leave, Mr. Bassey. Now I am telling you. If you are not out of here in two seconds I am going to call my father." She knew Big Rim was mad as hell.

She said, "And don't come back." She walked over and caught me by the arm and said, "Are you all right, Frankie? Can I get you something?"

I said, "No, I'll be all right. I don't want to cause anyone any trouble. I'll be going home soon. Thanks anyway." I gave her a half smile.

She smiled back and said, "This won't happen again, I am sure."

I said, "Well, I won't be coming back up here after I finish this job."

I looked around and saw Big Rim heading back through the hedges where he had parked his pickup truck. He got in and left in a hurry. Emily had left and gone back into the house. I finally finished up the job and started putting the tools away. All I could think of was getting the hell away from up there.

After I got all the tools put away, I headed for the front gates. Big Rim overtook me before I got there.

He said, "Get on back."

I said, "If you don't mind I'd just as soon walk."

He said, "Well, I do mind, now hop on."

I didn't argue. I just junped on back of the truck. Big Rim turned around and headed over to the outside trustee area.

We reached the dorms and Big Rim said, "Okay, get down. Your things are inside. Be ready for work at one o'clock sharp."

He got back in the pickup truck and drove off.

I walked inside the dorm and there were some of the old fellows I hadn't seen in quite sometime. We all sat and shot the breeze for a little while. Then I told them where I had been working. They began to look from one to the other.

Mack said, "For your own good, Frankie, I hope you don't have to go back up there."

Gill said, "Nobody works around the warden's house long. For some reason or other Big Rim has them back inside the walls."

Shortstack said, "You can't stand a bust, Frankie. You only have one month to do and, man, you will be out of this Giant. Man, if you get busted, now, that means you will have to stay here another ninety days. And just as sure as you work at the warden's house, you are going to get busted."

I said, "Hey, fellows, I agree with you. I'd just as soon spend the rest of my time inside. Coming out here wasn't my idea."

Shortstack said, "Anybody for chow?" He looked at me and said, "Come on, Frankie, le's eat."

I said, "No thanks, fellows, I think I will just relax. Don't feel too good. Got lots to think about."

So they all left and went to chow. I stretched out on my bunk and went to sleep.

At one o'clock Big Rim was there, Johnny-on-the-spot. It was he who took the fellows back to work. All of the ones who were in that dorm worked at one of the high officers' houses. So we all loaded on back of the truck. I didn't know where I was going. I had finished the job at the warden's house. Each time Big Rim would get to one of the officers' houses someone would jump off. After they had all gotten off but me, Big Rim headed up toward the warden's house. The warden was waiting outside when we got there. He was standing with his hands on his hips. I began to wonder what had gone wrong. I noticed he had a frown on his face. I looked over at the logs; they were still in place.

When we stopped, Big Rim told me to get off. Just as I got down, Captain Roundside drove up. The warden said, "Frankie, you go with Captain Roundside. He needs a good man this afternoon."

He turned to Big Rim and said, "Lieutenant Bassey, I want to talk to you . . . not after awhile, but now."

I got on the back of Captain Roundside's truck and he

pulled off. When I looked back, I could see the warden shaking his finger in Big Rim's face. Then I thought about what Emily had said. She must have kept her word, because Big Rim was catching hell from the warden.

Captain Roundside dropped me off at the motorpool. He said, "Go in and see Sergeant Lowsome. He needs somebody to drive the truck this afternoon. You can drive a truck, can't you, Frankie?"

I said, "Yes, sir. Anything on wheels."

He laughed and said, "I'll pick you up this evening around four-thirty."

I went inside the motorpool and for a few minutes just looked around.

Joe said, "Who are you looking for, Frankie?"

I said, "Sergeant Lowsome."

He pointed to a little office up front.

I knocked on the door and Sergeant Lowsome waved for me to come in. He was on the phone. When he hung up I told him what Captain Roundside had said.

He said, "Got a name?"

I said, "24357."

He said, "Not number, name. Out here we call people by their names. Now let's try again."

I said, "Hold on, no use. I am Frank Jackson. They call me Frankie."

He said, "Well, now, that's good enough for me. I need somebody to pick up the milk crew. Go over there and tell Old Dexter you are the one that's going to pick up the milk crew. He'll give you a trip ticket to get out of the gate with." I went over and picked up the trip ticket and headed out for the farm.

On the way out I began to think about what had happened at the warden's house that morning. And after I had kept my cool for eight years, nobody was going to make me blow it now, with only twenty-nine more days to go. I could stand on my head that long.

I picked the crew up and headed back to the prison. I dropped the men off at the dorm and took the truck back to the motorpool. I had some time left before Captain Roundside would be picking me up, so I got the water hose and washed the truck.

At four-thirty, Captain Roundside was there to pick me up. He took me over to the dorm. When I got there the rest of the fellows had made it in. When I walked in the door, Gill said, "You're just in time to join us for chow. I am hungry as hell. They worked the hell out of me today." I went and washed up and we all headed to chow.

After we had finished and returned to the dorm, I stretched out on my bunk.

Shortstack came over and said, "Hey, Frankie, I was wondering, would you do me a favor?"

I said, "Sure, Shortstack, just name it."

He said, "In the evening we usually have a little basketball game. My side has been on the losing end for quite sometime, so I was wondering, would you fill in for me this evening?"

I said, "Sure, anything for a pal."

He said, "My team seems to think that I am the cause of them losing so much. You see I don't rebound too good, and the fellows said they are tired of stepping on me so much."

We both laughed.

He said, "Thanks, Frankie, remember I owe you one."

So for the next hour and a half we played basketball. And at the end my team won. Gill and Mack came over and handed me a pack of cigarettes apiece.

I said, "Hey, what's the smokes for?"

Joe said, "Man, did Shortstack tell you everything about the game? We play a pack a man."

I said, "Well, that puts Shortstack five packs up on you guys."

Shortstack said, "Hey, fellows, I thought you were tired of stepping on me, so I hired Frankie."

I took the smokes and flipped them over to Shortstack. We both laughed. But the rest of the crew was mad. Shortstack and I went in and took a shower. After I had finished my shower, I came back to my bunk and started relaxing for the evening. The guard came to the door and said, "Mail call." I didn't get up. I knew there wasn't any for me. My mail list had broken off long ago. My wife had gotten a divorce, and the few friends I knew had long forgotten about me. So while the other guys were getting their mail I settled back on my bed and start reading a book.

Over across the walls, I could hear Leo putting those other cats to bed. Boy, he was laying some heavy blues on those cats. I was half reading my book and half listening to Leo. That's how it went until the guard came in and said, "Okay, fellows, lights out. I'll give you five minutes more, but no more." I took the book and laid it on the floor beside my bunk. Got up and took my clothes off and hit the sack. I drifted off to sleep listening to Leo putting those cats to bed inside the walls. A few of the other guys were digging it, too.

The next morning just before work call, I was told over the P.A. system to report to operation headquarters.

I looked at Mack and said, "Well, I guess I'll know where I will be working soon."

He said, "For your sake, I hope it's not the warden's house. From what happened yesterday, Big Rim is going to have it in for you. He was shooting his mouth off yesterday down at the motorpool and got a big laugh from his buddies. Two of our guys overheard the conversation. Big Rim doesn't like anyone working around the warden's house—and *that* you already know. I hate to see you get a bum rap with so little time to go, Frankie."

I said, "Thanks, Mack, but I finished that job at the warden's house yesterday."

I left the dorm heading for the O.H. When I got there, I met Sergeant Lovelace; he was standing out front.

He said, "Are you Frankie?"

I said yes.

He said, "Captain Roundside wants to see you in his office. But offhand I'll say you are going to work for the warden. But you better go in and get it from Captain Roundside. Just knock on his door, he's expecting you."

When I knocked, Captain Roundside said, "Come on in, Frankie. Well, Frankie, the warden called this morning and told me to send you over to his place. He also told me to sign you to his house for the rest of the time you've got here."

I said, "Captain, I am not going to refuse to go to work up there, but do you think you could get him to get himself another man? You see, sir, I know working up there means trouble from Big Rim. You know he busts every man who works at the warden's house. I only got twenty-nine more days to go, and I don't want no trouble, even if I have to go back in the walls. Maybe you could call hi—"

He cut me off. He said, "Frankie, the warden is not a man you question his orders. That's if you want your job. And I happen to want mine. I've been with the warden for fifteen years, and I learned fourteen and eleven months ago not to question his orders. Now if you got a problem, you had better take it up with him yourself. Now that's all. Big Rim is waiting for you outside."

I said, "Yes, sir," and walked out.

I didn't see Big Rim outside, so I started out walking. I wanted to think about what I was going to tell the warden. My thoughts were interrupted when Big Rim pulled up alongside of me. Then he cut the truck right across in front of me.

He said, "Where in the hell do you think you are going?"

I said, "To the warden's house."

He said, "What for?"

I said, "Captain Roundside sent me. He told me the warden was waiting for me."

He said, "Okay, move along."

He never moved the truck. I had to go around it. I never said anything more, I just walked around the truck.

When I reached the warden's house he was waiting outside.

He said, "Good morning, Frankie."

I said, "Good morning, warden."

He said, "First, let me thank you for the job you did on the logs. They look real good."

I said, "Thanks."

He said, "I guess you want to know why I sent for you? Well come on inside, my wife will show you. She has some work she wants done."

I couldn't bring myself to tell him I didn't want to work at his house. I just followed him inside.

Once inside, he said, "Have a seat, Frankie. The wife will be with you in a minute."

Then he left the room.

I took a long look around, and boy was it a fancy pad. I hadn't seen a place decorated like that in over eight years. Everything was far advanced on me. I said to myself, *Frankie you have been locked up too long. Things do change.*

The warden and his wife returned to the room. I stood up. The warden said, "Frankie, this is my wife, Mrs. Bolden." He told his wife, "Baby, this is Frankie, the one I told you about."

She said, "How are you, Frankie? Lloyd told me how you stopped him from letting the kids play on those logs before you had a chance to restack them. I want to thank you for that."

I said, "It's okay."

The warden said, "Well, I am going to leave you two alone. It's my work time."

He gave Mrs. Bolden a kiss on the cheek and left.

She said, "Would you like to have some coffee?"

I said, "Oh, no thanks. I had some already."

She said, "Well, I think I will. Come on in the kitchen and over my coffee I'll tell you what I want done."

I said, "Yes, ma'am," then followed her into the kitchen.

She said, "I want all the furniture in the living room moved to the center of the floor. Ever do any painting?" I almost lied and said no, but I was afraid the warden might have looked at my record. I was once part owner in a decorating company. She said, "I want all the old paper stripped off and the walls repainted. I want you to take your time and do it right. I'll be leaving in a little bit for town to start selecting some paint. I haven't made up my mind what color I want. Emily and Tony are still asleep. Don't mind them. They know you will be in here working. There will be some coffee in the pot, if you should want some. So help yourself. Don't try to do it all in one day. Take your time. Any questions?"

I said, "Yes, ma'am, just one, when do I start?"

She smiled and said, "I'll get out of your way."

I said, "You won't mind if I turn on some good music. I work better with that."

She said, "Not at all, just help yourself."

She started for the door and turned around, and said, "There is a key on top of the ice box to the tool shed. When Emily wakes up give it to her and tell her her dad said get another one made."

I said, "Yes, ma'am."

She said, "See you after awhile." Then she was gone.

I got the key and headed outside to get some tools. When I opened the door I saw Big Rim leaning up against the shed.

I didn't say a word. I just walked right up to the door and started unlocking it.

He said, "Where are you working at?"

I said, "Inside the house."

He said, "Doing what?"

I said, "Why don't you come inside and see?"

He said, "Don't get smart."

I said, "Right now I'm moving some furniture. I am going to do some painting later."

He said, "When you go inside you leave that back door open. I want to see you working when I make my rounds."

I said, "You got it, boss." I got what things I needed and started for the house. I left the door open like he said. Then I heard him say, "You remember what I told you yesterday—I'll be watching you all the time."

Just as I started moving the furniture, Emily came into the room.

She said, "Good morning."

I didn't even look at her. I said, "Good morning."

She said, "I am sorry for what happened yesterday."

I said, "That's all right. Thanks anyway."

She said, "Where is mother?"

I said, "She went to the store to get some paint." I still hadn't looked up.

She said, "Frankie, are you angry with me?"

I said, "No, not at all ma'am."

She said, "You don't have to say ma'am to me."

Then she walked over by the door that was open. I stopped working for the first time. I looked straight at her and said, "Look, ma'am, I am trying to do twenty-nine more days. I've been here long enough, I want out. Big Rim busted my gut yesterday for taking a drink of water from you. Now ain't no telling what would happen if he caught me talking to you inside your house. So I'd just as soon you didn't talk to me. In fact I have work to do. And your mother wants it done." I turned and went up the ladder.

She said, "Well, all I wanted to do was tell you I am sorry for what happened yesterday."

I said, "Now, you told me. Now why don't you just run

along before it happens again. Then you won't have to come around tomorrow telling me you are sorry again."

That made her mad. She was trying to say something, but I cut her off. I said, "Your mother said get a key made off of this one." I tossed her the key.

She stomped out of the room saying, "Men are all alike, you just can't please them." She went back into her bedroom and slammed the door. I knew she was mad as hell, but I had to get away somehow. Knowing that Big Rim was somewhere outside and the back door was open.

She didn't come back into the room, and I was glad. So I just kept on stripping paper off the walls. I went back up the ladder so I could get to the ceiling.

Just a little before ten o'clock Mrs. Bolden came back. She went to the kitchen and returned with two cups of coffee.

She said, "Come on down off that ladder and let's have some coffee. I don't like to waste my coffee."

I could tell from the tone of her voice that I better not argue with her. So I just crawled down and took one of the cups from her.

I said, "Thanks."

She took a look around the room and said, "Not bad, not bad at all." She said, "Come on over here and sit down."

I said, "Thanks."

She said, "Hmm, you have some courtesy about you, too. Don't get that around here everyday. All the other fellows who worked up here thought I was the cause of them being here. Come on drink your coffee before it gets cold." She got up and said, "Excuse me, I got to wake that boy up. If I don't he'll be there all day."

I finished my coffee while she was gone and went back upon the ladder and started stripping paper. I had worked about an hour and a half when Emily came back into the room.

She said "Big Rim is out front waiting for you. Don't you know it's lunch time?"

She gave me a towel and face cloth.

I said, "Thanks."

She said, "You can use the bathroom to wash up." Then she left the room.

After I had put the tools away and washed up, I started for the door. Emily was standing right in the doorway.

She said, "I am not moving until you tell me you're not mad."

I looked over her shoulder and Big Rim was taking it all in.

I said, "If it will make you happy, no I am not angry at you. Now will you get out of my way?"

She said, "You sure?"

I said, "I am sure." Then I gave her a big smile. I said, "Now will you move before Big Rim blows up?"

She said, "Okay." She was all smiles.

Big Rim jammed down on the horn. Then yelled out, "Are you going?"

I had to squeeze past her. She was laughing out loud then. Big Rim had blown up big as a bull. I ran over and jumped on back of the truck. Big Rim left there like a bat out of hell. I looked back and Emily was waving her hand. I pretended that I didn't see her.

When I reached the dorm, Shortstack and Gill were on their way to chow.

I said, "Hold on fellows and I'll join you."

Shortstack said, "We thought you were going to have lunch with the warden."

They both laughed.

We had all finished eating lunch and were back at the dorm sitting around shooting the breeze.

Joe said, "How is it going, Frankie?"

I said, "Not so bad. Big Rim was by today to remind me that I would get the same treatment I got yesterday if I didn't keep that back door open so he can come by and look in when he's making checks."

Joe said, "Whatever you do, Frankie, you watch yourself. The last guy who worked for the warden told us how Big Rim used to hang around at the back of the warden's house throughout the day. I made a few passes that way today, and he was hanging around out back both times I was by. I didn't stop to see what he was doing. I don't know what he's up to, Frankie, but whatever it is, watch yourself. I can feel that Big Rim is up to something no good. And one other thing, he is stuck on the warden's daughter, and she won't have anything to do with him. That's why it makes him boiling mad when he sees one of us working up there. And now you are working inside the house, that's enough to run the poor guy nuts."

I said, "Maybe he is and maybe he isn't. But thanks for the tip."

Joe got up and left. I sat there letting the thought go around and around in my head.

My thought was interrupted by Big Rim blowing his horn. I looked at my watch and it was one o'clock on the dot. So we all loaded on back of the pickup and left. I was the last one to get off, although I should have been first. Everybody looked at me when Big Rim passed up the warden's house.

After dropping off all the other fellows, he headed back toward the warden's house. After we reached the house, Big Rim got out and came around to the back of the truck.

He said, "Look, boy, if Mrs. Bolden leaves this afternoon, I want you to open that back door. And I will be by every half hour to check on you. So you be somewhere I can see you. Now get going."

I said, "Look Lieutenant Bassey, I got quite a bit of work to do, so why don't you come on inside and make the check?"

He got mad.

He said, "Look, the warden don't want me coming—you . . . you just never mind, and do like I said. Goddammit, don't give me any of your lip. Now get a move on."

He got in the truck and left.

I walked around to the back door and knocked.

Mrs. Bolden said, "Come on in, Frankie. Tony and I were just getting ready to leave. We should be back shortly. But what I wanted to tell you is, before you start painting, I want you to strip this hallway between the living room and the kitchen. Emily has gone already. When she comes back, tell her that Tony and I went down to the store and we will be back as soon as we are done."

I said, "Yes, ma'am."

Then she and Tony were gone.

I walked over and opened the back door like Big Rim had said. Then I turned the radio on that was on top of the ice box.

Wasn't long before I had some bad blues going. I went up the ladder and started working. After a few minutes I remembered what Big Rim had said. So I came down and walked over to the back door and took a look out. No Big Rim. I said to myself, to the hell with him, if he wants to know where I am, let him come inside. The warden must not want him inside the house, that's why he wanted the back door open. Damn him.

I went back up the ladder and started stripping paper off the wall. I had been working for a good hour and I hadn't gone to the back door to make a check. So when I started off the ladder, I heard Emily coming in the front door.

She came over to where I was and said, "Hi."

I said, "Hi, your mother told me to tell you that she and Tony went downtown, and they will be back shortly."

She said, "Thanks, see you later. I got to change clothes."

Then she darted out of the room. I went back up the ladder and started stripping again.

I must have worked about forty-five minutes. I decided to come down and check to see if Big Rim was outside. As my foot reached the last rung the lights went out on me. I was hit on the back of the head with something hard. And that's all I could remember. When I did come around, I was in a daze. Everything was going 'round and 'round. Far away I could hear people talking. Lots of people. The shape I was in and from the little view I did have, it looked like there were hundreds of people. I kept shaking my head, trying to clear things up for a better view. Suddenly I could see Lieutenant Mason real good. Far from him were more uniforms, and they weren't all prison guard clothes.

Lieutenant Mason said, "Okay, get your clothes on."

I felt my legs, they were bare.

I said, "What's going on, Lieutenant Mason? What happened to my clothes? Somebody hit me over the head."

He said, "Good, too bad they didn't tear it off your shoulders for you."

About that time one of the guards hit me in the face with my pants.

He said, "There they are. Now get up and get them on."

I looked around the room.

I said, "I don't remember coming in here. I didn't have any work to do in here. I was working in the—"

Lieutenant Mason cut me off. He said, "Shut up and get your clothes on and get the hell out of here."

When I did get my clothes on, I got to my feet. I looked out the door behind Lieutenant Mason. Right outside the door was Emily lying on the floor.

I said, "What happened to the warden's daughter? What's going on here?"

By that time Lieutenant Mason caught me by the arm and gave me a shove out the door. I was still dazed, and with the shove Lieutenant Mason gave me, I tumbled down the steps and landed on the ground. Two guards grabbed an arm apiece. They dragged me over to the back of a pickup truck. Two more guards got hold of me, and all four of them threw me up in the back of the truck. Three of them got in behind me, and all three started working me over. And, boy, did they do a good job of it. The last I remembered is that we were going through the front gates. When I came to, we had made it to the corner pocket area. I was holding my ribs.

I said, "Would you fellows mind telling me why all the rough stuff?"

One of the guards said, "Open your mouth one more time and I'll stuff my foot in it."

I took him at his word and didn't open my mouth. They had already proved to me they could be rough, and I didn't see any reason to press the issue any further, being that I was getting the worst end of everything, so I just set back, holding my guts, wondering what in the hell went wrong, and why. I knew that we had stopped in front of the corner pocket, and from the way things had been going, that was my next home.

I was helped out of the truck, but not like a lady. When I hit the ground, I was dragged inside by both arms. When they got through dragging me, they threw me in on the floor of one of those old iron cells. It felt like it hadn't been swept out in ten years.

I lay there for a little while before I tried to move. I was in quite a bit of pain. I don't know how long I lay there, but when I tried to move, I felt like I was coming apart. So I decided to lie still a little while longer.

My mind was trying to recount what had happened, and the only thing that would come to me was, when I was coming down off the ladder. I got almost to the bottom rung and somebody hit me over the head with something hard. And the lights went out.

I took my hand and felt my face. It was swollen bad. I rolled over and sat up against the wall. That felt a little better. My eyes were almost shut. I was still in a daze. Across the room I could see a bunk. It looked like it was a hundred miles away and walking. Somehow I made my way to it and crawled upon it. I rolled over on my back. With the pains, I must have passed out again, because when I woke up it was dark. The pains had eased up a little, but my eyes were open so I could see a little better.

I finally sat up and put my feet over the side of the bunk. Outside the cell door I could see by the one light in the hall. I made my way over to the sink. Just above it was a small light. When I turned the light on, there was a mirror made out of steel. I started the water running. I washed my face and took a look at it in the mirror. Boy, I didn't believe it was me. I took both hands and held some water to my face. Boy that sure felt good. Then I held my head under the water for a long time; that felt better. I took off my T-shirt and soaked it. Then I lay back across the bunk with the T-shirt across my face. Boy, that really felt good.

I kept wondering why in the hell my clothes were off when I was knocked out at the warden's house. Then I remembered Emily lying on the floor half dressed. That's when it hit me. She had been raped, and they were thinking I am the one who did it. I straightened up on the bunk. Somehow the pains didn't hurt anymore. I just sat there thinking to myself. *My god no.* They couldn't think that I raped the warden's daughter. I got up and walked over to the cell door. I had to talk to somebody, I didn't give a damn who, just somebody. I looked around the cell for something to make some noise with. I had to get somebody's attention. I didn't care who, so long as I could tell them I didn't do it.

I looked underneath the bunk, and there was an old tin coffee cup. I got the cup and started raking it across the cell door. Then I began to yell for a guard. In my emotion, raking the cup on the bars and calling for a guard, I could hear myself saying over and over, "I didn't do it, I didn't do it." *My god, why don't somebody come down here. Anybody, please come down here.*

Soon I realized no one heard me but the bars and the walls around me. I could hear the hallway repeating every word I said. Finally I gave up and sat down right by the cell door, holding on to the bars. I could feel pains coming back.

I must have fallen asleep sitting there, because when I woke up, a sharp object was pounding away in my rib cage. Then I felt a hard object punching away at my stomach. I looked up and there stood one of the guards. He was just about to give me a good one. I moved just in time. I got to my feet.

I said, "Look, officer, I got to talk to the warden. I didn't touch the warden's daughter. You've got to believe me. I didn't even go near her room. You tell him I want to talk to him."

He and the other guard who had just walked up just stood there looking at me. The one that punched me in the ribs said, "You know, he is still alive. Now don't you just wish we had the keys." They both grinned.

I said, "How long are you guys going to keep me in this here hole?"

He said, "Until you rot."

Sergeant Moore walked up with a tray in his hands. He said, "Don't worry, the buzzards want you when you get out of here."

I said, "Sergeant Moore, I got to talk to the warden. Look I know what you are thinking, but I didn't—"

He cut me off. "Forget it, Frankie, I just want to be there when they hang you, you miserable son-of-a-bitch."

I said, "Is she—?"

He cut me off again. "No, she's not dead. Now don't that make you very unhappy? I give you one thing for credit, you tried hard enough, but you missed. The job wasn't quite finished. She came to, but she don't remember anything. But don't worry, the doctor said she will be alright. Just takes a little time."

Under my breath I said, *Thank God.*

Sergeant Moore looked at the other guards.

He said, "Hey, fellows, how do dogs eat their food?"

One said, "Anyway they can get it."

About that time Segeant Moore took his hand and threw the food off the tray onto the floor. He looked at me and said, "Don't worry, you'll get hungry enough to eat it." They all laughed and walked away. He was right. I didn't realize just how hungry I was, until later when I woke up.

I took out the sandwich, which I stuck under my mattress earlier. I tried to take a bit, but I discovered that my jaw was too painful to chew it. So I picked the potatoes up off the floor and picked the dirt out of them as best as I could. Somehow I got them down. I took the bread and put it in my mouth and held it there until it got soft. Somehow I made out a meal. The meat I would try later. Meanwhile, I had to get a message out to the warden. I couldn't think of anything right then, so I crawled back upon the bunk and went to sleep.

The next morning I didn't see or hear anyone. I was hungry as hell, then I remembered the piece of meat I had put away. I got it out and tried to eat it again. This time I tried chewing it on my front teeth. It worked. It was rough going, but it worked.

I called out for someone. I was hoping someone was locked up in the corner pocket besides me. No luck. Seems I was the only one in the old hell-hole called the corner pocket. So I decided to let time play with itself.

Later, I had guessed it to be around noon, I was lying back on the bunk when I heard the big door open. I sat up on the bunk. I didn't know who it was. I thought it was that same crew that had been out there before. I got back on the bunk so they couldn't hit me. A few seconds later Captain Bennett and Lieutenant Thompson walked up to the cell door, followed by the guard who had been with Sergeant Moore when they tried to poke me in the ribs.

Captain Bennett said, "Okay, Frankie, on your feet."

I said, "Go ahead and talk, I'd just as soon sit here and listen to what you got to say. You see, Captain, I am a little sore from the treatment your yard dogs gave me yesterday. And don't mind if I don't speak too clearly; your yard dogs brought a dentist along with them. And what the hell all the rough treatment is about, I goddamn sure don't know. So if you got something to say, go ahead, I still can hear."

The guard, who was out there before, said, "Captain, I'll

get the keys from the tower guard. I know how to make him stand up."

Captain Bennett said, "No, let him be." He took a long look at me before speaking. Finally he said, "So that's the thanks the warden gets for giving you a break? He should have listened to me in the beginning, none of this would have happened."

I said, "Maybe not with me being the fall guy, but you can bet your ass it was going to happen someday. It won't be any use in telling you I didn't do it, will it?"

He said, "Not on your life."

I said, "I didn't think you would believe me. But now that we got that asked and answered, I won't cause my mouth any more bad pains by trying to convince you otherwise. But I would like to know just why in the hell did you come down here in the first place? Just to see if your yard dogs did a good enough job on me?"

Lieutenant Thompson said, "Now you just watch your mouth, boy."

I said, "What will you do, Lieutenant Thompson, lock me up in the corner pocket? I am already here. Or will you have your yard dogs work me over? But I've had that, too. Feed me one meal a day? I only get one now, and I have to pick that one up off the floor where Sergeant Moore throws it. You see, Captain, I began to get just a little bit displeased. Goddammit, I don't know why in the hell I am locked up in the first place, but I am. I get the hell beat out of me for something I didn't do. Now no one wants to listen. Now you come out here, Lieutenant Thompson, wanting me to be nice to the captain. Well, goddamn you and the captain, and the rest of you fucking pigs. I want to talk to the warden. To hell with the rest of you bums."

Suddenly everything got quiet. Captain Bennett was the first to speak. He said, "Why don't you sign a statement admitting you did it, it would go much easier on you."

I said, "Now that we are back on the crime in question, would you please tell me just what in the hell I am supposed to admit that I did."

Lieutenant Thompson and Captain Bennett looked at each other. Finally Captain Bennett said, "How about raping the warden's daughter for a start?"

I said, "Did you get Big Rim to sign one, too? That bastard

should be the one locked up out here instead of me. No thanks, Captain Bennett. But you can tell the warden, if he has the guts he can come down here and talk to me. He's the only one I want to talk to. And one other thing, tell Sergeant Moore, it doesn't matter about him throwing my food on the floor, I'll somehow make good of it."

Lieutenant Thompson and Captain Bennett looked around at the guard. He was looking like he had got caught stealing cookies.

He said, "Captain, it was Sergeant Moore's idea. He did it."

Captain Bennett and Lt. Thompson took a look inside the cell. I thought for a moment the guard was going to run.

Captain Bennett said, "Let's go."

I lay back on the bunk. I said to myself, "To hell with you, Captain Bennett, and your whole damn crew." *No way in hell would I sign a piece of paper saying I raped the warden's daughter, just to keep the heat off that goddamn Big Rim and your ass.* I quickly threw the thought out of my mind. I had to think of some way to get a message out to the warden. I lay back on the bunk and closed my eyes and started thinking.

I sat there a little while before I opened my eyes, and when I did, I looked up on the wall and there it was, a picture of a half naked woman. It had been torn, but the idea hit me. Now if it only worked. I carefully removed the picture from the wall. Then I took off my shoes. The idea was to rub my shoe sole on the floor until it got hot, then make my marking. Somehow it had to work. The message I wanted on the paper was, "paper and pencil, corner pocket." I knew it would be a long way around, but it had to work, so I went over and started working on it.

After about an hour I had it done. I took a look at it and it wasn't too bad. Not the best, but not bad. I knew it wouldn't take but just one convict to spot it and they would try like hell to get the paper and pencil to me, and if he couldn't he would see that someone else would. No convict would sit by and let you burn, especially when you're up against someone running the Giant. If someone could help you without getting himself involved, man, you got it.

I put the note under the bunk and waited for the next feeding. I had it all figured out on how I was going to try getting it out, and how it would make it. It depended on how sharp the guards were. It was getting late in the evening and I knew I wouldn't be getting anymore food before the next day.

Every hour on the hour, some guard would come by and check the cell by shining a light in on me, and they would try to hit me right in the face with the spot so it would wake me up. After they would succeed with their little game, they would walk on.

The night went by fast. When morning came, the guards made their rounds as usual. The rest of the morning I didn't see anyone. I paced up and down the cell to pass the time away.

I had just settled down for a little rest when I heard the door open. It was Sergeant Moore with another guard. He took the tray and shoved it under the cell door.

He said, "Don't think this letting you eat off a tray is my idea. I was getting a right good kick out of seeing you eat off the floor, and if I had my way, you wouldn't eat at all."

I said, "Thanks, sergeant, sometimes we just can't have our ways, now can we?" Then I reached down and picked up the tray. "Right now you would just love to have your way, wouldn't you, sergeant?"

He never answered. He and the other guard just walked away.

The food was just an old-time corner pocket special (peanut butter and jelly alone, with cold coffee, and, believe it or not, a wooden spoon). I fixed me a sandwich leaving just enough jelly on the tray to do what I wanted to do, then I laid the sandwich aside. I took the wooden spoon and spread the jelly on the bottom of the tray. I reached under the bunk and got the note, then I stuck it to the bottom of the tray and shoved it out from under the cell door. I settled back and began to enjoy the only meal I knew I would be getting before the next day.

A few minutes later Sergeant Moore came by to pick up the tray. I didn't look up at him. I didn't want to show any suspicion of anything. He bent down and picked up the tray and walked away without saying a word. I settled back for a long wait.

If the message got caught before it got to one of the other

inmates, I'd be the first to know. Somehow the guards get a kick out of letting you know they have broken up your little games, especially when you were trying to get the game by them.

Now, if the guard didn't catch it, it would just be a matter of time before I would hear from someone, somehow.

I couldn't sleep, so I got up and started pacing up and down the cell. Somehow time goes by faster that way.

The evening and night went by pretty fast. The guards made their regular rounds and played their little games.

The daylight was just beginning to peek through, then suddenly the door opened. I held my breath. I just knew that they were coming to tell me that my note didn't get out. I could just see them holding it up in front of my face and laughing. The thought made me mad. I was thinking of something dirty to say. Just before they reached the cell door, I heard one of them say, "Boy, this is a hell hole, I couldn't live in here. This is the worst they can do to a man."

The other one said, "Oh, what the hell, they deserve it. To do what this son of a bitch did, he especially doesn't deserve anything better. They should stuff his balls down his throat."

Just about that time they both reached the cell door. I pretended that I was asleep. They walked up to the cell door, took a look inside and left. Somehow I felt my chances were still alive, because if the note had been found, these two birds would have known it.

At the noon-time feeding, Sergeant Moore was there with my chow tray. He shoved the tray under the door. He walked away without saying a word. As Sergeant Moore was leaving, Captain Bennett and Lieutenant Bateman came to the door. They, neither, said a word. They took a look inside and kept on going. I never stopped eating. Boy, I was as hungry as hell. I didn't take time to find out what they had brought me. In fact, I didn't care so long as it was food.

After they had closed the door, I stopped eating long enough to feel under the tray for my note. Nothing. Suddenly the hungry feeling was gone and I couldn't eat. But I knew I would be hungry as hell before I got fed the next day, so I took what was left and put it aside.

A few minutes later Sergeant Moore came back in and

picked up the tray. Again he didn't say a word. I got up and started walking back and forth. I was trying to put together another thought of how to get another message out. No answer would come, so I gave up and lay down. Leo always told me that good things come to those who wait, and if you had a little music to go along with the waiting, whatever you were worrying about would come around.

So that night I drifted off to sleep thinking and humming one of Leo's old blues songs. Somehow I could hear Leo's guitar playing the background on some of those troubled blues, even though he wasn't anywhere around. And the song I loved to hear him play most was, "As the Night Keeps on Rolling." I must have slept through both the evening and late-night checks, because when I woke up the daylight had broken through. I got my snack out and started eating. Still no word from the outside.

I tried to think of some way to get another message out. After I had sat there for a little while, I heard the door open. I got up and walked over to the door. It was one of the guards. He came down and stood in front of the cell door. He was slapping his nightstick in his hand. I said, "Good Morning." He never said a word, just stood looking at me like I was something from outer space.

I said, "How is the warden's daughter?"

The expression changed on his face.

I said, "Well, I hope she's doing okay."

I jerked my hands off the bars just in time to keep him from breaking my fingers. He lunged forward trying to poke me in the face. I caught hold of the nightstick and gave it a yank. That caused him to get a pretty good bump against the bars. I caught hold of his arm and bent it backwards until the nightstick fell to the floor. He couldn't move.

I said, "Now you look here, you dirty son of a bitch, how would you like someone coming by poking you in the face when you can't fight back? What did you do, bet some other screw that you would sneak out here and bust my face? Well, you lost the bet, buddy. I should break your goddamn arm."

Then I tightened my grip up just a little more. I took my free hand and reached down and picked up the nightstick.

Then I gave him a hard shove. He almost fell to the floor. I took the nightstick and threw it at him, hitting him in the back.

I said, "Now get the hell out of here."

He picked up the nightstick, holding his shoulder.

He said, "You'll pay for this. I'll see to it that you pay. Next time I come down here I'll have the keys, then I'll see just how smart you are."

I said, "You do that, but right now do me a favor and get the hell out of here, you're making my stomach hurt."

He gave me a long look, then picked up his hat and nightstick and left, holding his shoulder. He was saying something I couldn't understand. I didn't know what was going on outside, but I had a feeling that they were trying to stick it to me, whatever it was.

Time was dragging by slowly. Noon finally came, and Sergeant Moore was back with my tray. I wasn't looking for anything until the next day. He sat the tray down and pushed it under the cell door. He stood there for a few seconds, not saying a word. I didn't get up. I knew he had heard by now what had happened between me and the other guard, to I didn't give him a chance to make up for that, and I just sat there. He looked a little disappointed. Then the thought hit me. I was not supposed to get another tray until the next day, so by him bringing me a tray, he just might get a chance to rap me one while I'm picking up the tray. I didn't fall for it, so he left. I reached down and picked up the tray and started eating without looking underneath it.

When I finished eating I sat the tray back down on the floor and lay back on the bunk, looking up at the ceiling. I was thinking about what had happened and how I was railroaded out to the corner pocket. The thought made me mad. I said a few choice words to myself.

I got up and walked over to the cell door. On the way I took my foot and kicked the tray all the way back to the back of the cell, then turned around and caught hold of the bars. I stood holding the bars until the main door opened. I backed away from the door. When I turned around, I couldn't believe my eyes. The tray had landed upside down and taped to the bottom was a piece of paper. I rushed over and ripped the paper off and stuck it under my covers before anyone could see it.

Sergeant Moore made it to the cell door and said, "You know you weren't supposed to get a tray this afternoon."

I said, "I'm sorry, but it's too late now. Somehow I think you knew it all along. You were hoping I'd reach down and pick it up in front of you so you could carry out your friend's little deal he made. Well, go back and tell him it didn't work, either." The tray was still lying at the back of the cell.

He said, "Bring your tray up here."

I lay down on the bed, leaned over, and placed the tray flat on the floor. Then I aimed at the bottom of the cell door and gave it a hard push. It landed right where he could pick it up. He gave me a dirty look, reached down, and picked up the tray and left.

I waited until the door was closed, then I took the paper from under the covers. Taped to it was a pen. Folded up were three sheets of paper. There was a note inside. It said, "Play one for you tonight." Without a doubt I knew it was from Leo. I said, "Old Leo came through."

I got down on the floor and began to write a letter to the warden. This is the way it went:

> Warden, you know as well as I do that I didn't rape your daughter. Big Rim set the whole thing up when he ordered me to leave your back door open while I was inside working. I was busy working when the whole thing happened. I was coming down off the ladder and had almost made it to the bottom when I was hit over the head by Big Rim. He went in and raped your daughter and tried to kill her so she wouldn't tell on him. He took my pants off while I was passed out. You know Big Rim has been stuck on your daughter for some time, and that's why he won't let anyone work around your house.
>
> Now if Emily is suffering from shock, she can be shocked out of it just as she was shocked into it. Check it out with your doctor.
>
> I know you must think I'm crazy to ask you to let me talk to Emily, but that is the only way I know how to help her. If I was the one that raped her, do you think I would be trying to get her to come around to put the finger on me?

So for the last time, I didn't rape your daughter. Now if you have the guts to come down here and face me after the way Captain Bennett and his other yard dogs have treated me, I'll still help Emily.

And I want you to know that it will be for Emily only. I don't give a God-damn what happens to the rest of your crew, including you. So if you decide to come down, let me know ahead of time so I can wait around for you. See you later, Frankie.

I stood up and walked back and forth, reading the letter. I was pleased with it, so I folded it up and stuck it under the cover to wait for the next feeding, which wouldn't be until noon the next day.

I had begun to get a little slack from not having enough food to eat. I hadn't had a shave since I was locked up here in the corner pocket, but, as always, there was one thing that could put my mind at ease, and that was to start humming one of Leo's tunes. It worked. Before long I was fast asleep. The next morning, long before chow time, two guards came in. I lay still. I recognized one of the guards' voices. He was the one who tried to break my hand on the bars with the nightstick.

I couldn't make out what they were saying, but I knew they were up to something. Whatever they were talking about, I was included in it, so just to make sure, I crawled down to the other end of the bunk. About that time they walked up to the cell door and in came a bucket of water. The water got all over me and the bunk. I couldn't do anything to defend myself. I called them a few dirty names. They just stood there laughing. The one I knew said, "Now sleep in that, you miserable bastard." They both left laughing.

At chow time Sergeant Moore brought down my tray and slid it under the cell door. He knew about the water.

He said, "What's the matter, the bunk getting too hard to sleep on, or did you have a leaking last night in your sleep?" He laughed and walked away.

I didn't say anything. I just got my tray and started to eat my meal, what little there was. When I finished I took the note from under the cover and used the same tape that Leo used and taped it to the tray. I set the tray down and slid it back under the cell door.

Sergeant Moore came back and picked up the tray without looking under it. He was too busy laughing at my having to sleep on the floor. I just settled back for the long wait to come, one way or another.

I knew the whole ordeal was hard on the other fellows who worked at the officers' houses, and if it hadn't been for that Goddamn Big Rim, none of this shit would be going on. He was the cause of it all.

I knew the ones who worked at the houses wouldn't be working there anymore. The people would be too afraid, and that son of a bitch was behind the whole damn thing. The thought was making me mad.

The warden's daughter wouldn't have the bastard, so he raped her. Now I'm suffering for it, locked up down here in the dirtiest Goddamn hole in the Giant, starving my ass off, all for nothing. And he's running loose. By then I was so mad I began to pound my fists on the wall. It wasn't getting me anywhere, so I pulled the pillow off the bunk and settled for a hard bed on the floor.

For the next few days things didn't get any different, only me getting weaker and my beard getting longer. And I still hadn't heard from the warden. Not a word. I began to think my letter didn't get out.

I had just taken out another piece of paper and had started another letter when I heard the door open. I took the paper and put it under the covers. I set up on the side of the bunk looking down at the floor. Then I heard a voie ask, "Where is he?" I knew the voice. I couldn't believe it. It was the warden. Captain Bennett said, "Right this way, warden." I said to myself, *Good God, my letter made it.*

I didn't get up, I just sat there with my fingers threaded together.

The warden walked up to the door and said, "Frankie?"

I said, "It's me. Surprised that I am still alive?"

Captain Bennett said, "Stand on your feet when you talk to the warden."

I didn't move.

Captain Bennett said, "You heard me, dammit, now get on your feet."

I said, "You will have to forgive me, warden, for not standing. You see I am a little weak from eating so much. And I don't feel like standing up. So if you have anything to say, go right ahead—I'll listen. I think I can hear just as good sitting down. You know, out here, warden, you only get one meal a day. And then somebody forgets to put something on your tray every time."

Captain Bennett and Lieutenant Wilson both looked at each other.

I said, "And you see, warden, I've been out here now for twelve days. That means I've been hungry for twelve days. So if you have anything to say, go right ahead and talk, I promise I won't leave until you are finished."

Lieutenant Wilson said, "Warden, we know how to deal with his kind."

The warden said, "Why don't you two step outside for a minute or two. I want to talk to Frankie alone."

Captain Bennett said, "Sir, you can't deal with that guy. You—"

Before he could finish, the warden said, "Captain Bennett I asked you and Lieutenant Wilson to wait outside. Now, dammit, I am telling you. Get the hell out of here, now."

With that note, they both left.

The warden looked at me and said, "I got your letter."

He turned around and took a look at Captain Bennett and Lieutenant Wilson and said, "And close the door behind you." Then he turned back to me and said, "How did you get the note out, Frankie?"

I said, "Now , warden, that's not a fair question. You don't expect me to let you in on that one, do you? After all I might just have to use that same route again."

He smiled and said, "I guess I should have known better than to ask you that."

I said, "How's your daughter?"

He waited a long time before answering. Then he said, "Not so good. The blow to the head left her in pretty bad shape.

The doctor says she's got a chance to make it, providing she regains consciousness. She's very lucky."

I said, "Do you still think I did it?"

For a moment he didn't say anything. Then slowly he said, "No, I don't think so, Frankie."

I said, "It was Big Rim, wasn't it?"

He said, "Without Emily we have no proof. So far everything points to you."

I said, "What about the suggestion I made in the letter?"

He said, "I talked with the doctor and he says it's a fifty-fifty chance."

I said, "What the hell kind of chance does she have now? Fifty-fifty is better than nothing."

He said, "Yes, I know . But with the way they treated you, I was wondering would you still go along with it?"

I said, "Sure, I'll go along with anything so long as it helps Emily. It will be for Emily only, no other Goddamn soul, that's including you, too, warden. Why in the hell isn't Big Rim locked up? He's the bastard that should be locked out of circulation. Sooner or later you will have one of the other fellows down here for something else he done. Whose daughter is he setting his eyes on now?"

I was getting mad as hell.

He said, "There won't be any next time."

I said, "And just what makes you think it won't be Snowflakes, Gill, Mack, or Bobby. They all work out there. You can bet there will be another one so long as that son of a bitch is running loose."

He looked down at the floor and said, "They all have been sent back to the walls, Frankie."

I said, "You said what? What happened to them?"

He said, "They were all sent back to the walls. Looks like when something like this happens, people get scared. The women don't want any of the fellows working around their houses anymore. They took a petition around and they all signed it. There was nothing I could do about it. I know it wasn't fair to the rest of the fellows, but that's the way it went."

I said, "So that puts me on the other side with the other fellows. To all of them, I was the cause of them losing their outside jobs. If I had left those goddamn logs alone nothing like this ever would have happened. '"

He said, "Some of the fellows don't hold it against you, they don't think you did it. And one is Leo. He is the one who brought me the letter. Leo has been made outside trustee now, just to make the pickups and deliveries. As for Big Rim, he quit shortly after this happened. He took his two days off and hasn't been seen since, not even around Coolidge, where he lives."

I said, "But, warden, we need him to carry out the deal I had planned."

He said, "Yes, I know. That's why we worked out this little deal, that's if you would go along with it? It's up to you."

I sat up straight. I said, "Let's hear it."

He said, "First thing is, we can't call the police in on this because we don't have any proof. So that means we have to bring Big Rim back without bringing in the police."

I said, "Just how are you planning on doing that?"

He said, "You are going to bring him back."

I stood up.

He went on. "We have arranged for you to escape. Nobody knows about the plan but Captain Bennett, Captain Roundside, and Lieutenant Mason. Lieutenant Wilson doesn't even know."

I walked over to the cell door.

I said, "So that's it. If they try me, I get fifty years. If Emily dies, I'll get life. So either way it goes, I'll be here the rest of my life. Now that's not good enough for you. You'd rather have me dead. You come down here with your bleeding heart trying to brainwash me into going over the walls. I'll get killed in the process. Headlines read, 'Convict Frank Jackson, accused of raping the warden's daughter, gets killed trying to escape.' No thanks, warden, I'll take my chances in court. Now, if you don't mind, I'd just as soon be left alone."

He didn't say a word while I was giving him hell. He waited until I was finished.

He said, "Are you through?"

I didn't say anything.

He said, "It's no set-up, Frankie. Emily thought a lot of you, so did my wife. They wouldn't ever forgive me if I did something to you like that. I am not trying to get you hurt. I couldn't live with myself either."

I said, "How in the hell would Emily ever know? She's out of her hea—"

He cut in and said, "And may never get well. Is that what you were going to say? Well, maybe she won't, if you don't help."

I said, "Helping is one thing, getting myself killed is another one. I want to live."

He said, "Well, just like you said in the note, 'warden you have to trust me.' Well, I'm asking you the same thing. Trust me."

I said, "I need some time to think about it."

He said, "Go ahead and think about it; meanwhile, it will take that much longer for Emily to get well, and it will be that much harder on her recovering. And, one other thing, you'll be helping yourself, too."

I said, "How do you know I won't keep going once I am out?"

He said, "Beause you won't be helping Emily any. And inside of you there is some good."

I said, "And what makes you think I can find Big Rim?"

He smiled, then he said, "Because I know something about you that you don't want anybody else to know, especially anyone around here."

I said, "And just what is that?"

He said, "Let's start by calling you by your right name. Okay, Fred Jones?"

I stood up.

He said, "I kept it a secret from everyone. If the rest of the convicts would have known you were an ex-cop you wouldn't have lasted six months around here." He said, "Just for the record, let me bring you up-to-date on yourself. Five years before you came here, you were with the New Haven, Connecticut, Police Department. You quit and went in with William Hunt. You worked with him as a private investigator. You finally took a twenty-five-thousand-dollar payoff to drop a case. You headed for Las Vegas, Nevada. Lived it up pretty good. Changed your name to Frank Jackson. Am I right so far?"

I didn't say a word.

He went on, "You got rolled for about ten grand. You came to Arizona and went to work down in Tuscon for the State

Detective Agency, using the name of Frank Jackson. This time one of your clients ended up at the bottom of the Gila River. You were found in your hotel room with the briefcase handcuffed to your wrist. Twelve thousand dollars he had just drawn out of the bank in Casa Grande was found under your rug. You couldn't convince the jury you didn't do it, so here you are."

I said, "And you knew this all the time?"

He said, "Yes, I knew it all along. In fact, for eight years. So you see, Frankie, I don't have to set you up to get killed by escaping. All I have to do is let the word get around that you were an ex-cop, then turn you loose to the wolves. So while you are thinking about our deal, remember you only got three days. Oh, by the way, you'll be given three meals a day from now on. And don't worry, you'll have enough to eat."

He turned and walked away.

I was still sitting there puzzled at what the warden knew about my past. I didn't notice him when he returned.

He said, "I'll be back in three days to clue you in on what we have planned. See you then."

I said, "Yes, okay, see you then."

I didn't look up. I was still thinking about what he knew about my past, and me bringing back Big Rim. Why me? Why couldn't he just hire someone else and let me out of this damn hole? I couldn't think of a good answer, and I knew he was right about my past, all except the deal in Tuscon, Arizona. I was framed on that and now the courts knew it, too, after eight years. I said, "Ah, what the hell." I lay back on the bunk and went to sleep.

At six o'clock the next morning, Sergeant Davis woke me up with a tray in his hand.

He said, "Well, well, if it ain't my old pal Frankie. Thought I would give you a pretty good feeding this morning, might take some of the wrinkles out of your belly. Goddamn, if you don't look something awful. Maybe by noon I can scrape you up a blade or two, and if it's okay with Captain Bennett, I'll have Ollie to come out and cut your hair. I am not going to ask you why you are in here, it's none of my business. I already know what the rumors are. I was just told to give you a good feeding. See you at noon."

I said, "Thanks, Sergeant Davis."

Sergeant Davis was an alright guy. He didn't push too hard, and didn't mess you around. If you had something coming you got it. And if you fucked up on him, you can believe you were not going to talk your way out of it. Quite a few of the guys liked Sergeant Davis, even me. And for that reason, he didn't get along too well with the other officers. And he didn't give a damn either.

I began to eat. I had meat on the tray. Boy, I hadn't seen any meat in twelve days. So I settled back and gave it hell.

And that's how it went for the next three days. Three big meals a day. All I could eat. Sergeant Davis kept his promise about the blade and razor. But they wouldn't let anyone come down to cut my hair. Captain Bennett didn't want to arouse any suspicion among the rest of the fellows as to why I was being treated so good.

Sergeant Moore was relieved from coming out to the corner pocket. In fact, no one was allowed out there but Sergeant Davis.

It didn't seem so bad being down there, now that I was getting three meals a day and plenty each time.

On the night of the third day, Warden Bolden, Captain Bennett, Captain Roundside and Lieutenant Mason all came down to the corner pocket. They were outside my cell door before I knew it. The light was out and I was sleeping pretty good. Captain Roundside took his cell-door keys and banged on the cell door. I woke up and turned the light on. I walked over to the door where they were. Captain Bennett said to the warden, "I must say again, warden, I don't like the idea at all. It makes no sense to me to let this guy out. Who knows whether he will come—"

The warden said, "Again, Captain Bennett, I say I don't give a damn whether you like it or not. Just keep your opinion to yourself and your Goddamn mouth shut about the whole damn thing. Now is that understood?"

Captain Bennett said, "It's understood, but it's your ball game if something goes wrong."

The warden turned to me.

He said, "Now, Frankie, are you awake enough to listen?"

I said, "As awake as I'm ever going to be. I made up my

mind to go along, so I might as well listen to whatever the hell I'm getting into. Come on, lay it on me."

He reached over his shoulder and got the keys from Lieutenant Mason and opened the door and came inside and sat on the bunk beside me. He said, "Well, first thing, Frankie, is to get you back to your old name. So from now on you are Freddie, just like it used to be. Now that shouldn't be too hard for you to remember. Now the second part is, I'm going to have you moved out of the corner pocket. You will be living in cell block two. Your cell will be right next to the guard station. Lieutenant Bateman is also in on the deal. Now, you don't give Lieutenant Bateman any trouble, we need him bad. He has strict orders from me not to let you out of your cell. And you are to have no conversations with anyone at any time. And no convicts standing in front of your cell. You will be under twenty-four hours' watch. No contact with anyone but the officers. Button your lips and keep them that way. You won't be going to the chow hall either. All your meals will be brought to you by Sergeant Davis, and Sergeant Davis only, because he is to fix your meals in the chow hall himself. The cell block officer in charge will pick up your tray. Now, one other thing. There's a wall in back of your cell. Behind the wall is a hole. Hanging in that hole is a suit, white shirt, tie, and shoes. There's no hat. Don't look at it, don't check it, don't even look that way at it. As far as you know it's not back there. You'll be told when to use it.

"Now, in the morning your things will be put in the cell. You'll be picked up here and escorted to the cell block, so be ready to leave here around 5:00 A.M. That's all for now. Any questions?"

I said, "So far, no."

He got up and said, "See you in two days." He started to walk away but stopped. He looked back and said, "Are you still with me?"

I said, "So far we only got three meals a day, and a chance to move out of this damn hole. Sure I'm still with you. If I don't like it I can always come back down here and have one meal a day off the floor."

Then his face became hard as a nail. He said, "Don't you think for once that I'm going soft. I am only thinking of one thing, that's my daughter." He turned and started to walk away with the rest of them.

I said, "Hey, warden," he looked around. "I'm only doing it for one thing, too, and that's your daughter."

I could see his face soften.

I turned around and lay down on the bunk. There wasn't a whole lot to think about, but a Goddamn whole lot to worry about. And the first thing that was on my mind was, *was the whole thing on the up and up?* And if it was, where in the hell would I start looking for Big Rim? What in the hell would I do with him after I caught him? Tell him, "Hey, Big Rim, they want you to come back over to the Giant so the warden's daughter can identify you as the one that raped her." I said, "To hell with it, let the guys who thought up this whole damn deal come up with some good answers to start with." I reached back and turned the light out and went to sleep.

The next morning around 5:00 A.M., Sergeant Davis and Lieutenant Bateman came in. Sergeant Davis unlocked the door.

He said, "I don't know what happened, but I got orders to move you to cell block number two. Lieutenant Bateman will take it from there, so don't ask me because I don't know."

Lieutenant Bateman said, "Okay, outside." He closed the door and locked it. He turned to me and said, "Let's go."

I said, "Boy, it sure feels good to be out of this place."

Lieutenant Bateman said, "It's not my idea, I'd just as soon see you rot there."

I remembered what the warden had said about giving Lieutenant Bateman a hard time, so I kept my mouth shut.

On the way to the cell block I met some of the guys going to early chow. I didn't say anything to them. Steve said, "Well, well, there goes Father Time. Looks like we're going to have him around for a long time." I just gave him the finger and kept walking.

When we reached the cell block, Lieutenant Bateman took me directly to my cell, shoved me inside, and locked the door. I turned around and placed my hands on the bars. I tried to work the door open. It wouldn't move.

Lieutenant Bateman said, "Still don't trust the warden do you?"

I said, "Well, now, it doesn't hurt to check, does it?"

He walked over to the cell door and said, "To me you are nothing but a low down, dirty bastard. I just wish the warden had put you in some other cell block instead of this one. I want you to know that you are not liked by me, or any of the cons in here, and to let you know how I really feel, I hate your guts. All the fellows who used to work outside at the officers' houses are in this cell block, and I'd like nothing better than to turn them loose on your Goddamn ass. Then, on the other hand, you're not worth any guy spending an extra day for. A low down, son of a bitch who did what you did doesn't deserve any protection. No, you couldn't go outside like the other fellows, do your work, and come back, you had to have a piece from the warden's daughter. Well, now that you got it, I hope to hell it was worth it, because there will be no coming back for you." He then said, "You turn my stomach." He started walking away.

I said, "Lieutenant Bateman, now that you are done, would you believe that I don't know whether the warden's daughter is still a virgin or not?"

He said, "I thought you—are why—"

I said, "You thought. That's just why I am here, just because someone thought. No facts, just thoughts. And for your information, I didn't touch her. I was framed, and I don't give a Goddamn whether you believe me or not. You got a job to do, so do it, and keep your Goddamn thoughts to youself. I'm not in the mood to listen to them."

I walked away from the cell door and lay down on the bunk. I must say that bunk was much softer than the one I had been sleeping on. I fell asleep. No one bothered to wake me up for chow.

Around ten twenty-five, Lieutenant Bateman punched me in the side and woke me up.

He said, "Here, Captain Bennett sent them to you."

I said, "Thanks."

He said, "Don't thank me, thank Captain Bennett."

I said, "Well, it's good to be thought about once in a while."

I finished off the sandwiches and went back to bed.

The next morning, after all the guys had left out of the cell block for work call, I asked one of the guards to get me a razor blade.

He said, "Sure, if you promise me you will cut your throat with it, then I'll get you two."

I didn't ask him anymore. He finally walked over to the guard station and got me one and brought it back and laid it on the crosspiece between the bars. I picked it up and went back and started shaving. I had finished and was wiping my face when I heard Lieutenant Bateman saying, "Yes, sir, he's okay. No trouble at all, sir. Right this way, sir."

I turned around to see the warden standing in front of my cell door. He said, "How are you and Lieutenant Bateman getting along?"

I said, "Swell, sir. When he gets busted I'm going to have him for my cell partner." I looked over at Lieutenant Bateman. He was about to blow up. I winked my eye at him. Boy, he just about came apart.

The warden said, "Come over here, lieutenant, I want you and Freddie to get better aquainted." He put his arm around Lieutenant Bateman's shoulder. He said, "From now on things are going to depend on you two cooperating with each other."

Lieutenant Bateman said, "Are you still going to let him go, warden? After what he's done."

The warden said, "Now look here, lieutenant, you just hold on, I don't want to go through with you what I had to go through with Captain Bennett. Okay? Now, both of you listen, because this is what we have planned. This afternoon there will be fifteen people in here from the Department of Correction. Among the group, dressed in street clothes, will be Captain Roundside. Freddie, he will sign your name on the book. Lieutenant Bateman will let you know when they start coming in. You get dressed. Your door will be fixed so you can just slide it open. Lieutenant Bateman, you will make sure the rest of your men will be upstairs. The group will stop here last, on their way back out to the front gate. Captain Roundside will be at the end of the line. He will break off and go into the guard station. When the group makes it to the front gates, Captain Roundside will go to the yard offices. Freddie, you slide your door open and join in at the tail end of the group. Try not to hold any conversation with any of the men in the group. You go to the front of the crowd and try to be the first one to sign out under the name Fred Jones. And make it look a lot like what Captain Roundside has written. Now outside to your left of the gates, there's a new Chevrolet. It's white over blue. The keys are under the floor mat. The license number is written down at the check point, so you shouldn't have any trouble getting out. Don't speed going out and don't look at the guard at the check point. Now, once you pass that check point, the ballgame is on. Are there any questions so far?"

I said, "Just one. What will I do for I.D. in case I get stopped?"

He said, "Good question. In the glove box, there's an I.D. card with your name on it. And a few other things. In an envelope there's five thousand and five hundred dollars."

Lieutenant Bateman swallowed real hard.

The warden said, "There also is a gun in there."

Lieutenant Bateman just about turned white.

He said, "Yes, Lieutenant Bateman, Freddie used to be a cop, so don't, for once, think I'm crazy, because I'm not. I know what I'm doing, so you just go along with the idea, okay? And keep your mouth shut." Then he turned back to me. He said, "Okay, Freddie, you got two weeks to bring Big Rim back."

I said, "And if I don't, what then?"

The warden looked around and said, "As far as the Giant knows, you escaped. But in the meantime, you will turn yourself in to your contact man. Your contact man is Tim Duncan. If you know him already, that's better."

I said I didn't.

He said, "If there's trouble with the law, call this number, nine-eight-seven-ought-ought-ought-five. Just say four-two-six and hang up. You'll get a call back on the number you're at."

I said, "Any one place I might start looking for Big Rim?"

He said, "He lives in a little town not far from here called Coolidge. Now that's the best I can do. Good luck and good hunting."

He and Lieutenant Bateman started to walk off.

I said, "Warden, now that you know that I didn't harm your daughter, if I don't find Big Rim, and I return to the Giant, what happens then?"

He walked back to the cell door. He looked me straight in the eyes and said, "As for the moment, you are public enemy number one. Without something to prove you're not, we couldn't just go and disappoint everybody, now could we?"

I said, "I got the picture."

Lieutenant Bateman walked inside the guard station, looked around, scratching his head. Then he walked back around to the cell door and said, "I don't like this whole damn thing. Not even one bit. The whole damn thing stinks. Why in the hell should they go through all this for your ass? And now they want me to be a part of it, I don't like it."

I said, "You don't like it? How in the hell do you think I feel? If I don't go through with it, I spend the rest of my life in here for no Goddamn good reason. If I don't find Big Rim, I come back like a good boy and spend the rest of my life here. And even after I find the son of a bitch and bring him back, if the warden's daughter doesn't snap out of her spell, I still get charged with the beef and stay here the rest of my life. So what the Goddamn hell have you got to worry about? The warden asked you to turn your back and do a little dishonest thing just to help his daughter, and you might make captain out of it. If the whole damn thing blows up, nobody gets the shaft but me, not you, the warden, or any of the rest that's in on it. I get it. So don't come around here telling me what you like and don't like, I give less than a Goddamn. So do me a favor and get the hell away from in front of my door. Tell somebody else your troubles. I got some thinking to do." I turned and sat down on the bunk.

He said, "While you are thinking, think of how you are going to spend the rest of your life here."

By then I was pretty mad. And I knew *that* wasn't going to help matters at all, so I settled down and didn't say another word to him. One side of me was telling me to go ahead and blow my top. But blowing my top meant blowing the whole deal, and a chance to clear myself for good. I lit up a smoke and took a long drag off it and let it out slow. I heard some noise at the front of the cell block door. It was the work gang coming in for lunch. I had put a curtain up to my door. So I let it down as they were coming in. The way I was feeling right then, I didn't want to be bothered with anybody. They made a few catcalls my way as they were going to their cells.

I took a short nap while they were out to chow. I didn't

feel like eating. I was awakened when they were going back out to work call for the afternoon. I pulled the curtain back just in time to see Snowflakes and Shortstack going out on the gang. They both gave me the old finger. I closed the curtain back. I knew what they were thinking, that I was the cause of them being back inside the walls. And for what happened to the warden's daughter, they were no longer trustees. A step of what they called "precautionary." And they were suffering for that on account of me. So I guess they had reason to be angry at me.

After the building was cleared, Lieutenant Bateman came over to the cell door, and said, without pulling the curtain back, "Okay, Freddie, the ballgame has started."

That meant that the visitors had started coming in. Lieutenant Bateman sent the other two guards out to lunch. He told them not to return to the cell block until the visitors were gone. He said Sergeant Davis would be over to take me back to the corner pocket. Even though the old bastard wasn't any good, I had to give him credit, he could think straight. He wanted the other fellows to think I had been sent back to the corner pocket. And that's how they were going to account for my leaving the cell block.

I started changing my clothes. While I was changing clothes, Lieutenant Bateman was fixing the door so I could just slide it open with my hands when the right time came.

After we both had finished, Lieutenant Bateman walked over to the cell door. He said, "From now on, Freddie, the ballgame is all yours. I just hope the whole Goddamn thing blows up right in your face."

I said, "That's good. With you thinking that way, things just might work the other way. And if they do, just think, I won't have to put up with a son of a bitch like you anymore. Now that should make you proud. To yourself you will know that you are just as crooked as I am."

I reached down and got my shades and put them on. Then I checked myself out in the mirror. For a moment or two, I didn't believe it was me. I must say I didn't look too bad.

I closed the curtain and waited for the big move. If I say I wasn't scared I would be lying. I fired up a smoke and that did the job. About half way through the smoke, time came for the big move. The visitors had begun entering the cell block.

As they moved toward the rear, Lieutenant Bateman gave me the signal. I backed out of the cell and closed the door in front of me. I moved slowly toward the guard station. When I got there, I asked Lieutenant Bateman how I looked. He said, "So far so good." But he could see that I was a little shaky. He said, "Now, Goddammit, don't blow the damn thing right here." Then he said something that made me mad. He said, "With all that money you can buy yourself a piece of ass and you won't have to come back here raping the warden's daughter."

Suddenly the shakes were gone. I gritted my teeth and was just about to say something dirty. But when I looked around, the visitors had just about made it to us. He reached out his hand and said, "Good luck." I took his hand and gave it an extra squeeze. Then I fell in behind the rest of the crowd. I was behind all the rest as we approached the gates. I made my way to the front of the crowd.

When the gates opened, I was the first one to get to the signout book. I found my name, which had been written by Captain Roundside. I did my best to write like him. Wasn't too bad. At least the guy that was supposed to be checking us out didn't notice the difference. The tower guard counted us. When he was pleased with the count, he opened the door.

After I had gone about twenty feet from the gates, I looked to my left and there it was, a white-over-blue Chevrolet. I walked over and opened the door, got in, and found the keys and brought the engine to life. I backed out and got in line with the rest of the cars, almost to the last one. The first two cars were stopped at the check point. The guard took a quick look and waved them on. When I finally got to the check point he waved for me to go on. I began to unloose a little.

I reached the main street and turned left heading toward town. When I got to the outskirts of town I noticed a sign pointing to my left saying Coolidge, Arizona, ten miles. There was another one pointing in the same direction saying Phoenix, sixty-five miles.

I pulled over and stopped. I opened the glove box and took out the I.D. cards and put them in my pocket. Just ahead was a Y-formation. There was another sign pointing toward Tucson. I took out the money and counted it. Then I took out the I.D. cards and checked them. My old Social Security card was there, too. They had put it on a metal piece. I took another look at the signs ahead. The one that was pointing toward Tucson was getting tempting by the moment. My thoughts were broken when a sheriff's deputy pulled alongside me and asked if I was lost. I said, "No, I think I can make it. Thank you very much." He drove on. I said to myself, "What the hell am I thinking about. We made a deal, now why not stick to it." I brought the engine back to life. I took the turn pointing toward Coolidge.

After driving about fifteen minutes, I reached the main drag leading to downtown Coolidge. I stopped at a motel just on the outskirts of town. I pulled in the driveway of the DeLeo's Motel and parked. I got out and rang the bell. After a few seconds a little guy came to the door.

I said, "Got a room?"

He said, "For how many?"

I said, "For now, just me. If my luck holds out, I may have company later."

He said, "For how long?"

I said, "For right now, let's start with four days. If I need more time I'll let you know ahead of time."

He said, "That will be ten dollars a day, and if your luck holds out, there will be one dollar extra for the laundry, that is." He said, "What are you going to be doing in town?"

I said, "Does that go along with the room, too?"

He gave me a little dirty look.

I said, "No offense."

He turned to the wall and got the key and turned the book around and said, "Sign here."

While I was signing I said, "Are there any good places in town that a guy can get a bite to eat and a drink?"

He said, "Try the Double Tee Grill, real home cooking. And right around the corner is a place called the Check Inn, real nice." He said, "Maybe you won't have any trouble making your luck hold out there."

I said, "Thanks again."

He said, "There will be a twenty-five-dollar deposit, you can pick up the rest when you check out."

I took three tens and laid them on the counter and picked up the keys.

I said, "Which way?"

He came out from behind the counter and said, "This way, Mr. Jones. Oh, you forgot your change."

I said, "Keep it."

He put on a big grin and said, "Thanks."

He opened the door and showed me the room.

I got in my car and parked it in front of the room the clerk had pointed out to me. I got my bags and went inside.

I put the bags down and took a long look around the room. I said to myself, "When was the last time you were in a room like this?" I didn't know how in the hell the deal was going to come out, but it sure as hell was looking good from here. Even if I didn't catch that son of a bitch called Big Rim, I sure as hell was going to live it up and find me a broad.

I took my clothes off and went in and took me a long shower. When I finished, I walked around in the room. It was in the middle of the afternoon and the valley of the sun was at its peak. So I rolled the cover back and crawled into that soft bed. Boy, it felt like something I had been dreaming about for over eight years. So I closed my eyes and melted away.

When I woke up it was just a little after ten o'clock. I took a look outside. For a minute or two I thought I was in the middle of a fair with all the neon signs. I got up and washed my face and changed clothes. I must say the warden had good taste for clothes.

I headed out to find the eating place the clerk had told me about. My stomach had begun to talk back to me.

I found the Double Tee Grill with no problem at all. I went in and took a seat at the back so I could see the front door. I didn't want to get spotted by one of the guards. I knew that there were quite a few of them living in Coolidge. I used to hear them talking about the little town. I was just setting there thinking of how good it felt to be free. My spell was broken when the waitress came over to take my order. I ordered a steak, medium well, and all the trimmings.

After I had finished eating, I decided to drive around for a little while. I wanted the steak dinner to settle down before I had a drink. After about a half hour, I stopped in at the Check Inn. When I entered the door I took a quick look around. I didn't see anybody I knew, so I took a seat in the corner. When the barmaid came over, I ordered a double shot of Old Grand

Dad, one hundred proof, on the rocks. When the barmaid brought it over, I took the glass out of her hand before she could sit it down and turned it up and polished it off and handed her the glass and told her to do it again. She smiled and said, "My, you must be pretty dry." I gave her a half smile. She walked over to the bar and refilled the glass and brought it back. She handed it to me.

I said, "You can set that one down, I think I will let it cool a little." She smiled and walked back to the bar.

I had almost finished that one, too, when I noticed this real pretty woman seated to my left. Her glass was empty and she was rolling the ice cubes around in it with her finger. Her mind seemed to be working overtime. And she was staring into space. I didn't notice any other glass on the table, so I figured she was alone. I motioned for the barmaid. I said, "Whatever that lady in the yellow dress was drinking, give her another one. And do this up again, also." The little woman still hadn't broken her spell. When the barmaid brought the drink to her table, she set it down and pointed over toward me. I gave her my best smile. She smiled back. I thought that would break the spell. But she took one sip and went back into space. I picked up my drink and walked over to her table. She didn't look up. I took my glass and tapped on the table. When I got her attention, I pointed to the empty chair across from her.

I said, "Do you mind?"

She said, "No." Then took another sip out of the glass.

I said, "Is he coming later?"

She said, "There's no he, I'm not expecting anyone."

I said, "Is there something wrong?"

She said, "No." Then took another sip from the glass.

I said, "Something you want to talk about?"

She started to her mouth with the glass but set it back down on the table. I had to take a second look. There were real tears rolling down her cheeks. For a moment I didn't say anything. I just sat there and watched her cry, then I reached into my pocket and gave her my pocket handkerchief.

I said, "Anything I can do?"

She said, "No, I'll be all right. I'm sorry."

I said, "That's all right. A good cry helps sometime. Do you live around here?"

She said, "No, just passing through. At least I was until yesterday."

I said, "What made you stay?"

She said, "My little boy."

I said, "Do you want to talk about it? Maybe it would help."

She said, "It really isn't anything."

I said, "Maybe if you talked about it, it wouldn't be as bad as you think it is. I am a good listener."

She smiled.

I said, "Come on, give."

She finished the rest of her drink. I motioned for the barmaid to bring us two more.

She said, "I haven't seen my father in over fifteen years. He lives in San Francisco. That's where I was going. Everything went fine all the way from Kansas City, Kansas, until yesterday."

I said, "What happened then?"

She said, "My little boy got sick and the doctor put him in the hospital. He's been in now for two days. I called my father in Frisco and I can't get hold of him. I don't know how I'm going to pay for his hospital and doctor bill, and the motel, too. I don't have enough money to hold out much longer. If only I could get hold of my dad." The water had sprung another leak. It was running like crazy. She said, "I had all this on my mind tonight, so I decided to get out and have a drink. I told Judy to take care of Bobby for a little while, so here I am."

I studied her face for a moment. She didn't look like the type that went around putting the bite on men with sad stories. Hers was too real, and too easy to check out. I sat back and let her sob for a minute or two. That was the only way I could get her to talk without the sobbing. It never took me long to figure out whether a person was lying or not, and she wasn't lying by any means.

When she finally got control of herself, I said, "Freddie is what they call me. Fred Jones is my real name."

She said, "I'm Toni, Toni Mattin." She said, "Look, I don't mean to bore you with my troubles. I admit I wanted someone to talk to, but I didn't mean to—"

I cut her off. I said, "You're not boring me. After all I was the one who asked you to spill it all out. Look, how long did you say your boy has been in the hospital?"

She said, "Ricky, that's his name, he's been in two days, but that's not the point. He is to come home tomorrow, but I haven't got hold of my father so he can send me money. The doctor gave me these prescriptions to get filled. He said Ricky will have to start taking these as soon as he gets home, and I haven't filled them yet."

I said, "Do you have them with you?"

She said, "Yes."

She took them out of her purse. I picked them up and took a look at them.

I handed her one and said, "Write your address on the back and I'll deliver them tomorrow."

She said, "I can't let you do that."

I said, "I want to do it for Ricky. Now you wouldn't want him to come home and you don't have it, now would you? I won't take no for an answer."

She said, "You don't even know anything about me."

I said, "Sure I do. You are Toni Mattin. You have two sons, Bobby and Ricky. Ricky is in the hospital and you need to get this medication for him before he gets home. I am Fred Jones, who everybody calls Freddie. I want to help. So you see, I do know you. Now come on and scratch the address down so you can get home to Bobby. He's missed you about now."

I gave her a pen and she started writing down the address. When she finished I took the paper and put it in my pocket.

She said, "This, I just can't believe. I didn't expect you to do all this."

I said, "Look, you get out of here and go see about Bobby and quit worrying about other things. Come on, get. Tomororw I'll drop the medication off at your place."

She was all smiles. She still couldn't believe it was happening. I stood up and took her by the hand and led her out the door to her car.

She said, "If my dad doesn't send me the money, how will I pay you back?"

I said, "We'll cross that bridge when it comes. Right now quit griping. Good night. I'll see you tomorrow."

I opened the door so she could get in. I closed the door

and walked away. When I got to the door I turned around and waved at her. She brought the engine to life and drove off. She honked the horn and waved. I walked back inside the bar and ordered another drink. This time I sat at the bar. When the barmaid brought it, I said, "What's my bill?"

She said, "Six-twenty-five."

I laid a ten on the counter and said, "Keep the change." Her eyes lit up like a pinball machine. I said, to myself, *What the hell, helping the lady out, shit, it was state money. They were the ones footing the bill. Hell, if I don't find Big Rim I go back to prison and the money goes back to the state. Hell, let somebody be happy with some of it.* I finished off my drink and walked out.

I got in my car and drove around until I found a telephone booth. I got the phone book and started looking for Rim Bassey. After about a minute or so I found what I was looking for. I took out my pad and pencil and wrote down the number. Then I found a dime and dropped it in the phone and dialed the number. The phone rang about three times before a woman's voice answered.

I said, "I would like to speak to Mr. Bassey, please."

She said, "No one lives here by that name."

Before I could get in another question, she hung up. I stood there shuffling the receiver in my hand. Somehow I had the feeling either he was there and didn't want anyone to know it, or she had been instructed to tell anyone that asked for him that he didn't live there. The more I thought about it, the more my mind was racing on why he wouldn't answer his calls. And just maybe she could be telling the truth.

First he raped the warden's daughter and put the blame on me and then quit. Left the prison without letting anyone know. Maybe he found out that she was still alive and was going to talk. Now he's gone into hiding. He knew she hadn't put the finger on him yet because the police weren't looking for him. Maybe he was going to hide out until they nailed me to the cross. That would set him scot-free. He knew the state wouldn't reopen the case just to prove a convict is innocent. They would just insist on Big Rim's resignation, give him his retirement he had saved up, and close the case. I would be the one that had to rot out the time in prison. I told myself that I had very little time to lay a hand on Big Rim, and standing there wasn't doing any good.

On my way back to the motel, I stopped and picked up a fifth of Old Grand Dad, 100 proof. I needed a drink so I could do some thinking.

I got to the motel, went in, kicked off my shoes, got me a glass, and poured me a good glass of whiskey and drank it down. I sat on the side of the bed trying to put together something to start on.

Soon I found myself thinking about Toni and little Ricky. I said, "What the hell am I thinking about them for when I got my own troubles to be worrying about? Hell, that's what got me into all this shit in the beginning, trying to be a good guy, thinking about what could happen to the warden's kids if they got on those logs and they started rolling. What was it going to take to make me keep my nose out of where it doesn't belong?" I said, "Oh, what the hell," and poured another drink. Hell, I had already promised her I would do it. I didn't know a damn thing about her, but I'd do it. I set the glass down, pulled off my clohtes, hit the sack, and turned the light out.

At eight o'clock the next morning I was up and showered. About half way through shaving, there was a knock at the door. I said, "Now just who in the hell could that be? Nobody knows where I'm staying." I opened the door to find it was the clerk.

He said, "Hi, got a message for you. The man that left it said to be sure to call. That sounded like him calling a little while ago, but I wouldn't connect him to your phone."

I reached in my pocket and handed him a buck and said thanks. I closed the door and opened the envelope. It was from my contact man, Tim Duncan. I said, "How in the hell did he know where I was staying? I wasn't supposed to contact him until I found Big Rim." I folded the note and put it in my pocket. I went in and finished shaving and got dressed. I said, "To hell with him." I had something else to do. I headed for the drugstore. It didn't take long to find a drugstore. I went in and gave the man the prescriptions. He took a look at them and said, "It will be a few minutes." I asked him was there a telephone in the house? He pointed to the corner.

I dropped a dime in the phone and dialed the number on the note. It was picked up on the first ring.

I said, "Freddie, what can I do for you?"

He said, "Something new came up yesterday. Thought you should know about it."

For a few seconds I didn't say a word. My mind was trying to figure out what could have happened I should know about.

He said, "Hey, are you still there?"

I said, "Sure, sure I'm here. Did something happen to the warden's daughter?"

He said, "No, man, be cool, you're still in the ballgame. It's about Big Rim."

I said, "What about Big Rim?"

He said, "Somebody turned in Big Rim's resignation papers yesterday. He's changed his address to a P.O. box number. The number is six hunred forty-three. And one other thing, have you got the morning paper?"

I said, "No, I haven't."

He said, "Well, just the same, you went on the prison escape list yesterday, too." He said, "Don't worry, the warden didn't put out the posse. You were last seen boarding a plane that was bound for New York. The story is in the morning paper.

"Now here is one other thing, don't go around Big Rim's house. They have a feeling that he is trying to leave for Mexico. The heat is on and it is staked out. That's all for now. If I need you, I'll call you."

I said, "How in the hell am I supposed to—." The phone went click. I said, "Hello, hello," but there was no answer. I stood there squeezing the receiver in my hand. I said a few nasty words and slammed the receiver down.

I walked over to the counter and got a paper. Sure enough, there was the story on the front page. "Convict Accused of Raping the Warden's Daughter Escapes." I gave the lady behind the counter a dime.

She said, "They should catch that guy and hang him without a trial. Don't you think so?"

I said, "You bet I do, and I'm going to help them."

She said, "What?"

I said, "I'll help them."

She was about to say something else when I walked over to the counter to get the prescriptions. I asked the guy how much did I owe him? He said, "They are pretty expensive, twenty-one dollars and forty cents." I gave him a dirty look. He said, "Sorry, that's what the doctor ordered."

I said, "For that, would you tell me where the post office is located?"

He said, "Yes, about five doors down the street."

I paid him and walked out.

I took a walk down to the post office and had a look around. I asked the clerk did they have all the morning mail put away? He said, "No, it will be another forty-five minutes."

I said, "I'll be back."

I made a walk down the hall where the boxes were. I found #643 and looked through the glass. The mail was still in it.

I got in the car and headed over to Toni's house. Her place wasn't too hard to find. I parked the car and walked down until I found her number. Just before I rang the doorbell, I took a long breath of that bacon she was cooking. Boy, it sure smelled good. I knocked on the door and stepped back. The curtain opened and some other woman opened the door.

I said, "Miss Mattin?"

She said, "Oh, you must be Freddie. Come on in. She's been expecting you." She said, "Have a seat. Toni will be right out. She's fixing breakfast. Have you had breakfast yet?"

I said, "No, but I'm not going to stay long."

About that time Toni came out. I had to arrange my eyes for a second look. Was this the Toni I met last night?

She said, "Good morning."

I said, "Good morning."

I was trying to get to my feet.

She said, "Keep your seat. Won't you have some breakfast with us? I cooked plenty."

Before I could answer, she said, "Sure you will, and I won't take no for an answer."

I held out the paper bag.

She said, "Gee, I don't know how to thank you."

I said, "Then don't, I'll take it out in breakfast."

She said, "Freddie, this is Gloria. Gloria, Freddie."

They were all smiles and very happy.

The spell was broken by little Bobby. He came over to me and said, "Is Ricky going to be all right?"

I said, "You bet he is. I brought him some medicine that is going to have him running all over the place."

Toni said, "Bobby, I told you to get washed up for breakfast."

He was a little happy, too.

She looked at me and said, "Come on, it's getting cold."

I knew I was in for a good meal. I got up and went in and washed up. When I came out Toni said, "How do you like your eggs?"

I said, "Anyway I can get them."

She said, "Oh, come on."

I said, "Over light will do."

What she didn't realy know was that for the last eight years I had been getting powdered eggs. I really didn't care if these broke on the plate.

I sat down and dug in with the rest. Boy, I was giving everything hell. I looked over and there was only one biscuit left on the platter. I looked up and everyone was looking at me. I reached over and took the last one. I said, "Remember, it was you who invited me." They all laughed.

After I finished, I walked over to the sink where Toni was running water.

I said, "I'm a good dishwasher

She said, "You'll do nothing of the kind. You've done enough already. I just don't know how to thank you."

I said, "Don't try."

I was standing very close to her.

She said, "Thanks anyway."

I said, "You are very much welcome. You'll be in Frisco before you know it."

I could feel the gaze was getting warmer.

She said, "Come on and sit down."

I said, "No, I hate to be the type that eats and runs, but I've really got some long, hard work ahead." I said, "Can I call you?"

She said, "Sure you can."

She left and wrote the number down.

When she brought it back I said, "I'll call you this evening."

She said, "Okay, I'll be looking forward to that."

I said, "And remember, I want to see Ricky before you leave."

She said, "You will. In fact, I'm picking him up this afternoon."

I walked over to the door and said, "Call you later," and left.

She walked to the door and said, "I'll be looking for your call."

Somehow I felt good, but I didn't have time to make romance. I had to find Big Rim. Getting involved with a broad would only delay my time, and speaking of time, hell, I only had three more days. I had to do some thinking, so I headed back to the motel. I parked and went inside and started pacing across the floor, like I had done in the cell. Finally I kicked off my shoes and lay across the bed. I began to think about what Tim had said.

I must have slept pretty hard, because when I woke up it was dark outside. I fumbled around until I found the light. I knew I had to start asking questions somewhere, so the Check Inn Lounge was as good as any. I got up and got dressed and headed down to the Check Inn.

I walked in and took a quick look around, didn't see anyone I knew, so I took a seat on the back part of the counter. I sat on a stool where I could see who came in the front door.

The barmaid didn't ask me what I wanted. When she came down she had a double shot of Old Grand Dad in her hand. She sat it down and stood by. I gave it the same treatment I had the night before. She went and got another one and sat it down and left. I took the glass and turned it up and finished if off. I motioned for her to bring me another one. When she set the glass down, I said, "Look, I'd like some information. That is if you can help."

She said, "I can't," and started to walk away.

I said, "It's very important."

She slowly walked back and looked me straight in the eyes, then she said, "Look, mister, if it's about your wife, I don't know her. If it's something somebody did, I didn't see it, and if you want to know where it happened, I wasn't there."

I took a twenty-dollar bill and put it on the bar.

I said, "It's a man. His name is Rim Bassey. Everybody calls him Big Rim. Do you know where I can find him?"

She looked around and answered a knock on the bar. Some guy wanted a beer.

She said, "Fold it real small and I'll be back. I got to wipe the counter off."

She finished getting the beer for the guy and got her towel and started wiping the bar off. When she got to me she mopped the twenty-dollar bill up and kept going. I finished my drink and ordered another one. She brought the drink and sat it down.

She said, "He used to come in here once in a while. Sometimes alone, and other times with two other guys who worked with him at the state prison. Haven't seen him around in the last two weeks now. Used to brag when he got one too many of how he was going to be the next warden. Used to talk something about being in the family. And always would brag about how pretty the warden's daughter was. He would say how much they were in love with each other, but she never came in here with him and the other fellows would say he was just full of wind.

"The word got out that some convict raped her, and what I hear now is that Rim almost flipped his lid. Nobody has seen hide nor hair of him since."

I said, "What about his folks?"

She said, "You want another drink?"

I downed what was left in the glass and handed it to her.

She went and got another one and sat it down.

I said, "His folks, do you know where I can find them?"

She just stood there wiping the counter. I reached in my pocket and took out another twenty-dollar bill and folded it and laid it on the counter. She mopped it up with the towel.

She said, "Got two brothers. One works for the police department here in town. The other one works for the sheriff's department over at Casa Grande. Never did know where he lived here in town."

I said thanks and started to walk out.

She said, "Hey, you haven't paid for your drinks yet."

I walked back and took a five-dollar bill and laid it on the counter.

She said, "That will be twenty-five cents more, sir."

I dug up the quarter and slapped it on the counter. I leaned over and whispered, "I hope the hell you choke on it." She gave me one of her best smiles and said, "Thank you, sir, come again." I gave her one of my best nasty looks and left.

I found the Double Tee Grill again, went in, and this time I took a seat at the counter. I ordered coffee and a piece of peach pie. I hadn't eaten a piece of pie that tasted that good in a long time. After about four good bites it was all gone. I ordered another one. This time I worked a little slower. About halfway through that piece, I began to get a little crowded on my left side. I looked around slowly. There was a tall, heavy built guy seated beside me. He ordered coffee. After the waitress brought his coffee, he took the cup in both hands and slowly moved it toward his mouth. About half way up he said, "Did you find out anything today?"

From the voice I could tell he was Tim Duncan. I began to get mad.

I said, "I thought I was supposed to get in touch with you if I needed you. I didn't know you were going to be following me around all over town."

He said, "Look, I'm getting news from back at the Giant. I try to pass it on to you, but you don't seem to like that idea. So far you haven't come up with a damn thing. You dig? So go on and eat your pie and listen."

He said, "Now I know how we were supposed to contact each other. That's out. The warden's daughter has begun to come around just a little, but not enough to clear you. So what we need to clear you is Big Rim. I figured if we joined forces we might bring him out of hiding. You realize that one tipoff that he is being hunted, and he is Mexico bound. And as for you, that's not even a good thought to think about. Now if we located him together, I've got a way to take him directly back to the warden. It will mean we have to run a tight risk, but I have an idea we can do it."

I said, "You are not thinking about kidnapping him are you?"

He said, "You know a better way? Look, we can drag him, carry him, run him, or even get behind him and walk him. I don't give a damn. Just so we get him back there. Look at it this way, Freddie: your chances are slim either way you look at it. The best thing you got going for you is that when Emily sees the bastard, she will snap out of her spell. At least you got that much working for you, because if she don't, man, you got troubles, big troubles, and you don't get another chance to prove yourself."

I said, "Well, why in the hell didn't the warden just let you bring him in?"

Tim sat his coffee down.

He said, "Well, Freddie, it's like this. The warden knows you didn't do it, but he can't convince the rest of those guys working for him of that, so the only way he could at least give you a chance to get out of it was to set up the deal he did. Now here is the big thing. If the deal falls through, don't try to run, 'cause if you do I'll have to stop you. Maybe we'll have a shoot-out and you'll get killed. Now that will be to Big Rim's advantage, and then he will go scot-free and the public will be pleased that you paid for something you didn't do. But no one will ever know that."

He took a sip from the coffee cup.

I said, "Just how in the hell do you know I won't kill you, now that I know all this?"

He said, "You want your freedom too bad and you're not a killer."

I said, "How much are they paying you for this job?"

He said, "Ten grand, and whatever you have left of that five thousand they staked you with—so spend lightly. Remember, you're spending my money."

At that time I was so Goddamn mad I could have blown his head off right there.

I said, "You're more of a son of a bitch than I thought you were."

He said, "Now, now, remember we are working together. We need each other. If I recall, you once made off with twenty-five Gs. Put a hole in the guy's boat, spiked his drink, and left him in the middle of the lake. Just happened two fishermen came along and saved the poor guy from drowning, so don't you sit there and call me dirty names. Just say we are two of a kind. I need the dough and you need your freedom. So you might say we need each other, so let's get down to business, okay?"

For a moment neither one of us said a word. Then I said, "What's your next move?" I said, "First, you got the story wrong about me and the boat and the twenty-five grand. I do admit that there were some illegal transactions, but not like the story you just told."

He said, "Just read the newspaper and your record. So what do you say, let's mop this case up and let you get the hell out of that miserable damn place."

He reached out his hand. I took it and gave it a squeeze.

Tim said, "Now, the way I've got it figured, Big Rim needs money. He has quite a bit that the state has been holding out, and he has put in for it. Now somebody has to pick it up at the post office. He's not going to take a chance on coming out of hiding. Not now. My first suggestion is to stake out the post office. You and I will take turns, unless you have a better idea."

I must say I didn't like the idea of being out in the open myself, but I guess we had to start somewhere. So I said, "What the hell, let's give it a shot."

Tim said, "I'll take the first watch." He got up to leave and then sat back down. He said, "I think I will have a piece of that peach pie. It looks good."

I told the waitress to bring me another one, too. We both had another cup of coffee, too.

When Tim finished he got up and said, "I'll see you tomorrow."

The waitress said, "Sir, you haven't paid for your order yet."

He told her, pointing to me, "He's taking care of the bill."

I said, "Look, I am not—"

He said, "Look, you got state money in your pockets, and I'm working for the state right now." He leaned over and said, "It's my money, anyway."

He winked his eye at the little lady and left.

I said, "You low down, dirty so—"

When I looked around, the little lady was looking me right in the eyes. I laid two dollars on the counter and gave her a smile and started to walk off. She said, "Sir, you had three pieces of pie, that will be two dollars and forty-five cents. Your friend had a slice of pie and two cups of coffee. That will be another one dollar and ten cents. Total, three dollars and fifty-five cents."

Right then I didn't like her either. I picked up the two dollars and laid a five on the counter.

I leaned over and said, "Go downtown tomorrow and buy yourself a new dress."

I turned and walked out. I got in the car and headed to the motel. I was parking the car when I heard the phone ringing. I rushed in and picked up the phone and said, "Hello."

Toni said, "Where in the world have you been? I've been trying to call you for the last two hours."

I said, "I had something very important to take care of."

She said, "It must have been pretty important."

I said, "You can bet it was. In fact, my life depends on it." I said, "By the way, are you alone? Don't answer that, just put some clothes on and meet me at the Check Inn." Before she could say anything I said, "See you in about a half hour," and hung up the phone. I went in and took a quick shower and changed clothes.

When I got to the Check Inn, I took a look around to make sure things were clear, then I started looking for Toni. She wasn't hard to spot. She was seated to my left in a bright red dress with white trimming. She was looking good. I walked over to the table and stood and took a better view.

She said, "Don't just stand there staring, sit down."

I said, "My, you sure are looking lovely tonight."

She said, "I feel great." She was all smiles.

I said, "Well, how are things going?"

She said, "Just great, thanks to you. And the second thing is, I heard from dad."

I said, "Great, are you leaving soon?"

She said, "Tomorrow morning. Daddy was out on a fishing trip and he just got back in town. He wired me some money. Now I can pay you back for what you did."

I said, "You'll do nothing of the kind."

I motioned for the barmaid.

She said, "Tonight I feel better than I've felt in a long time. Now, what about you?"

The smile on my face must not have fit me too well. She said, "Freddie, what's wrong?"

I said, "It's a long story. I'll be all right in a day or two."

She reached over and caught me on the arm and said, "You want to tell me about it?" Just about that time I spotted two of the prison guards coming in.

I said, "Somehow, I don't feel like drinking tonight. Would you like to go for a drive? It's a shame to waste such a lovely moon like the one out tonight."

She said, "If it will make you feel better, why not."

I put three dollars on the table and we left.

We got in my car and headed out of town into the desert. After about five miles, I turned off on a dirt road and continued driving. All the time Toni had been talking about how happy she was to leave and what she was going to do when she got to San Francisco. Also how Ricky was feeling. I stopped the car and pulled off the road into the desert. Suddenly she quit talking.

She said, "Why are we stopping here? Freddie, you haven't said a word since we left."

She said, "Are you listening to me?"

I said, "Yes, I'm listening."

I slowly turned toward her. I could feel the fright in her speech.

She said, "Freddie, don't you think we better be getting back? I left Gloria with the kids. You know—"

I cut her off. I said, "Toni, Toni, don't be afraid, I'm not going to hurt you. I just want to talk to someone. I knew if I had started telling you what I want you to know back in town, you'd never have stayed and heard me out. So don't fret, I couldn't hurt someone as lovely as you. So when I finish telling you what I want you to know, we will head back to town. Okay?"

She just bowed her head. I knew she was scared.

I said, "It's true my name is Fred Jones, and they call me Freddie. But there's something else about me I want you to know. Now are you ready?"

She just sat rubbing her hands and staring at me with wide eyes.

I said, "I guess you heard what happened to the warden's

daughter over at the state prison. Well, right now you are sitting alone with the one they accused of doing it. I'm a convict from the state prison."

She just about turned white.

She said, "Oh, my God, no. Please, can't we leave. Look I have some money, you can have it."

I said, "Will you just shut up for a minute or two and listen."

She was crying.

I said, "Toni, I didn't do it. And if I had I wouldn't be sitting here alone with you now. I know you are afraid, but I'm not going to hurt you. I just want you to hear me out, okay?"

She said, in a low whisper, "Okay."

I said, "Toni, one of the guards did it. And he put the blame on me. The warden knows I didn't do it, that's why I'm out now. He gave me a chance to prove I didn't do it, and a chance to bring the guy back that did it. I only have one chance to prove I didn't do it, Toni, and time is running out. And if I can't, I go back and spend the rest of my life in the prison. Now, you think you are afraid sitting here with me, you should feel how scared I am. The only chance I have the warden gave it to me. Now, if I was the one who raped his daughter, do you think he would let me out to find the guy?"

She said, "I just don't understand it."

I said, "The guard that did it is somewhere in town hiding out until he gets his money he has coming, and then he will split, and I'm left holding the bag. Toni, I've only got two more days to lay hands on him.

"The guard's name is Rim Bassey. They call him Big Rim. Right now I'm working with another guy named Tim Duncan. So far neither one of us have come up with a damn thing."

She began to ease up a little.

She said, "Why didn't the warden go to the police?"

I said, "He had no proof. It might sound funny, but we have to have Big Rim back at the scene of the crime before we can prove it. But the worst part of the deal is, it's a do-or-die for me. And I just found that out tonight from Tim. Just before you reached me at the motel I was having coffee with Tim, and he told me the other part of the deal. That just about blew me apart. If I don't find Big Rim, I go back to prison and spend the rest of my life there, because I can't prove I didn't do it. Or I can try to run and Tim has orders to kill me. That way the public will be pleased and the case will be closed."

She said, "Then what about Big Rim?"

I said, "He goes scot-free. He couldn't go back to work there, but he could go to another state and change his name and live a happy life. No one will think of reopening the case, again.

"So you see, Toni, I only have two days to find Big Rim and take him back. For the good it will help, that's how I ended up in the Giant in the first place. I was framed with some money belonging to a dead man planted in my apartment. I couldn't prove I was in the clear, so they sent me to prison for eight years. And just before this thing happened, I received a letter from the judge saying they had found the right man, and he ordered the warden to release me."

I reached in my pocket and gave her the paper. I turned the dome light on so she could read it. I said, "But to keep the judge in the clear, he ordered me released in thirty days.

"So you see, Toni, my life has been abused by mistakes made by other people."

She handed the letter back to me.

I said, "I didn't think it would be fair to keep the truth from you."

When I said that, I started the engine and turned the car around and headed back toward town.

For a long time she didn't say anything.

Finally she said, "Freddie, is there anything I can do?"

I said, "Yes, there is, tomorrow you take Bobby and little Ricky to San Francisco to see their grandfather, and forget about me."

She said, "I could get my daddy to get you a good lawyer."

I said, "A lawyer isn't what I need. Right now I need Big Rim."

She said, "I am sorry for the way I acted."

I said, "Don't be. If I was in your place and somebody got me out in the desert and told me he was a convict I'd feel the same way. You have a right to be afraid."

I got to the Check Inn and parked the car. I got out and

walked around to her side and opened the door. When she stepped out she was standing right against me.

She said, "Please, let me help, I don't want to leave you in this mess. Let me call my father and see what he can do."

I said, "Toni, I don't want you to get involved in this. Somebody like you deserves someone better. So if you really want to help, you can, by taking the boys to Frisco. Now go home and get a good night's sleep so you can get an early start."

I took her by the hand and walked her over to her car. When we reached the car, she turned around and put both arms around my neck and pressed her body close to mine. Her lips found mine, which wasn't too hard. For a moment I forgot about everything. I held her tight. Suddenly I let go and pushed her back.

She said, "Freddie, please."

I said, "No, now, good night."

She got in the car. When she turned around I could see the tears rolling down her cheeks. I took the back of my hand and wiped her face, then I took my thumb and mopped the bottom of her eyes. She held my hand and kissed the back of it. I took my hand away slowly and said, "Good night and good-bye, Toni." I turned and walked back to my car. I had to leave before I changed my mind. She started the motor and pulled off. I turned around and watched the taillights until she was out of sight. I walked back to my car and got in and headed back to the motel. I wanted to do some thinking.

I reached the motel and parked the car and got out and started fishing for my door keys. I found the key and unlocked the door. As soon as the door opened I smelled smoke. I reached for my gun. Then I heard a voice say, "My, do come in." I knew right away it was Tim.

He said, "You come in every night with your gun in your fist?"

I said, "Only when I know someone like you is in my room. And speaking of my room, just how in the hell did you get in?"

He said, "Freddie, you've been out of the game too long." He was spinning a ring of keys around his finger.

I said, "Okay, now just what in the hell do you want so bad that you had to break in? What's happening that they can't wait? Are they getting a little scared and want me out of the picture?" I still hadn't put my gun away.

He said, "Relax, Freddie. If I was going to make a hit on you I wouldn't do it in such a foolish way. Come on, put the hardware away. We've got some business to talk over, and to start with, you owe me twenty bucks."

I said, "Just what in the hell do I owe you twenty bucks for? I paid for your damn meal earlier tonight."

He said, "Well, first of all I drove around town half the night looking for you. No luck, so I stopped in at the Check Inn."

I said, "Don't say anymore. You had to fold it up small and lay it on the counter and when the old gal came along she mopped it up as she was cleaning the counter off. She returned and sold me out."

He said, "Right on." Then he held out his hand. "You know you've got state funds you haven't touched yet. No use in the state getting it all back."

I put the gun away and took twenty bucks from my pocket and slapped it in his hand.

I said, "I wasn't told I had to pay your way, too."

He said, "Now come on, Freddie, don't be that way. You know you can't spend all that five grand before we wrap this job up. What's left is mine anyway, so I'm just spending a little of my money in advance. Now can you dig it?

"Now, about the stake out. I'll take the first watch in the morning. My guess is that whoever picks up that mail will take it straight to him. Then I will contact you. Now, you stay here until I contact you, and if the deal doesn't go down, I'll contact you anyway. Okay?" He started for the door and then stopped. He said, "I know I haven't given you a real good reason to like me, Freddie, but I am giving this thing every effort until I get you out of this mess. Just hang in there and don't give up." Then he walked out the door.

I lit up a smoke and took a long drag off it and let it out slow, then I jammed the cigarette out. I took my clothes off and went to bed.

The next morning I was wakened by the telephone ringing. I picked the receiver up. It was Tim.

He said, "Forget about the stake out, Freddie. Today is a holiday. The post office will be closed. See you tomorrow." He hung up.

I got up and took a shower and dressed. I decided I was hungry. After I had stopped at the Bee's Place and eaten, I decided to drive around for a little while and ask questions.

I stopped at the corner where a group of young fellows were just passing the time away talking to each other.

I got out and said, "Anybody know where I might find Big Rim?"

Nobody said a word.

I said, "His name is Rim Bassey. Everyone around here calls him Big Rim."

Still no one said anything. I looked at my watch. It was a few minutes past eleven A.M. The valley of the sun was just getting into the 100s (hot), and I wasn't getting a damn mumble out of those guys. When I got back in the car, they all began to laugh.

I said, "Thanks for the information, fellows."

I decided to go by and say good-bye to Toni and the kids. When I got there her car was gone. I started to drive off when the door opened. It was Toni. I backed up and parked and got out. I walked up to the door and said, "I thought you were gone? Where is the car?"

She said, "Come in."

I said, "Where is Gloria and the boys?"

She said, "Why don't you sit down. I'll get you a glass of water."

I said, "I will when you start giving me some answers." I caught her by the arm and before she could walk away, I said, "Toni, you are trying very hard not to tell me something. Come on, let's have it. What's going on?" I said, "Maybe I should start over."

She said, "No, you don't have to. Gloria and the boys are gone. They left around four o'clock this morning. She turned her head.

I said, "Why didn't you go along, too." I took my finger and turned her head back around. She was crying.

She said, "I couldn't leave. I mean, not until you got this—well, I just thought—"

I said, "You don't have to explain anymore." I was holding her close to me then. I said, "I'm glad you didn't go."

She threw both arms around my neck. She was shaking all over. I found her lips. I kissed her for a long time. I took my foot and kicked the door shut. I reached down and picked her up in my arms and carried her into the bedroom. She didn't have anything on but the housecoat. I took my fingers and unbuttoned the housecoat and let it hit the floor. I was trying to kiss her while she was trying to unbutton my shirt. Somehow we managed to get out of the clothes. She got in bed and I slid in beside her.

She said, "Freddie."

I put my hand over her mouth and said, "Don't talk."

I kissed her lips lightly. I took one hand and was rolling the nipple of her breast in my fingers. She was moving more and more under every squeeze. She said in a low whisper, "Freddie, don't tease me anymore." I caught the end of her nipple in my lips and gave it a little bite. She took her foot and kicked the cover back. She never got her legs closed. I was on top of her. For the next few minutes, I was lost in the land of many dreams.

We both lay there breathing heavily and looking up at the ceiling.

Finally she turned to me and said, "Freddie, I didn't want to leave you here alone to face what you have to."

I said, "You crazy broad." I kissed her lightly on the lips. I said, "I'm glad you didn't go."

She said, "I wanted to help you. Before Gloria left I told her I was going to stay until you got everything cleared up. My dad will understand. So this morning, just after daybreak, I went looking for my uncle, Rim Bassey." For a moment I thought I was hearing things. She went on, "So I just got in town and went to the police station and asked where I could find Uncle Rim. The desk clerk told me he was living right up the street from here at the Gig's Motel, in apartment number eleven."

I sat up in bed.

I said, "You mean to tell me you found out where Big Rim is at?"

She said, "Sure."

She was pulling me back down in bed.

I said, "Cut it out, Toni. Are you sure you know what you're talking about?"

She said, "Sure I'm sure." She put her arm around my neck and said, "Don't worry, he won't be going anywhere. He's just right up the street." She said, "Come on don't leave."

I said, "Why in the hell didn't you tell me this in the first place?"

She said, "And miss the way I feel now? Not on your life."

I was reaching for my clothes while she was still fumbling around with other things.

I said, "Will you cut that out and let me get the hell out of here. How in the hell did you do something Tim and I couldn't do?"

She said, "Now you see, I don't even get a thanks." She smiled and said, "But I did get something."

I was trying to get my shoe on while Toni was running her hand under my shirt and rubbing my back.

I said, "Will you let me get dressed? I've got to get in touch with Tim."

I finally got her out of the way enough to get to the phone. I started dialing Tim's number. In two rings he answered the phone. I said, "Tim, I found out where Big Rim is. I'm at Toni's house. She lives at hello—hello—." He had hung up. I said, "What the hell, Tim hung up." I put the phone down and and went to the bathroom. I took a quick wash up and came back into the room. I got my shirt and went back into the bathroom to comb my hair. The door opened. It was Toni. She didn't have anything on. She just walked right past me into the shower and turned the water on. I was trying like hell to get out of there and she was laughing.

I said, "To hell with Tim. With or without him, I'm going to get Big Rim."

Suddenly I heard a knock on the door. I knew Toni couldn't get it.

I said, "Just a minute."

I fastened my pants and went to open the door. It was Tim. He was half dressed.

I said, "Come on in."

He said, "Where is Big Rim?"

I said, "Right up the street from here. Toni found him. I'll fill you in later."

I heard the water cut off and the bedroom door was open. I walked over and closed the door. Toni put her housecoat on and came into the room.

She said, "Hi, Tim."

He said, "Hello, Toni."

I said, "You two know each other?"

She said, "Yes, Tim came by and told me how bad you needed to find Big Rim so I told him I would stay and help. I didn't tell him how though."

Tim said, "I also found out about you and her with the double sawbuck, so what the hell, we'll get to that later. Right now let's go find Big Rim. Something tells me he won't be there too much longer."

Toni said, "You two are not going to leave me are you? After all, I did find him, you know."

I said, "No way. It's too dangerous."

She said, "Some two you two are. I do all your work and now I can't see the climax of the thing. Just do me a favor and get out of here."

I walked over and held her in my arms and said, "Toni, I know I won't see you anymore. It may not work out like we think it will, and you know what that means, but thanks for everything. I'll always remember you."

She said, "Go on and get out of here."

I knew she was crying. I gave her a quick kiss on the forehead and Tim and I left out the door. She walked over and slammed the door. We got in my car and headed for the Gig's Motel.

Tim said, "What's the hurry? We can't pick him up before night."

I said, "I want to make damn sure he is still there. And who says we can't pick him up before night?"

Tim said, "I said so. I made a deal with the warden that we would bring him after dark to keep you from getting spotted."

We reached the Gig's Motel and went inside. We didn't see

the clerk, so I started ringing the bell. Finally the clerk came out, wiping his hands.

I said, "Look, we are—"

Tim cut me off and said, "Looking for a double suite."

The clerk said, "For just the two of you?"

I said, "No, there's two more."

He said, "I have just one and it's thirty-five dollars a night."

Tim said, "Sounds good. We'll take it."

I said, "Is it already unlocked?"

He said, "My, my, no, we can't leave them open." He turned around to get the key.

Tim took the sign-in pad and turned it around. Sure enough, there was Rim Bassey, about the sixth one down—apartment number eleven.

When the clerk turned around with the key, Tim said, "Now, you sure you don't have anything else? The last time I was here I stayed in number ten."

He said, "I am sorry, but that's a single and it's already filled."

Tim said, "We really don't have to be in until tomorrow. Could I get the single one at number eleven for the night?"

The clerk said, "It will be a day or so before it will be empty. Mr. Bassey will be checking out then."

Tim reached in his pocket and took out a ten and laid it on the counter and said, "We'll be back after we talk to the girls. Thanks for the trouble." Tim handed him the ten spot.

He said, "Sure. Thanks a lot. You want me to hold it for you?"

Tim said, "No, we will be back for sure, but if somebody wants to rent it go on and let them have it."

I said, "See you later on."

He was surprised as hell.

He said, "Fellows, I'll be right here."

We both left.

We got in the car and headed up to my place. Tim hadn't said a word since we left.

After we got inside of my apartment, I said, "I don't know what it is, but come on let's have it."

Tim said, "There's nothing to tell."

I said, "Don't give me that, come on out with it."

He said, "I am just glad we caught up with him. Look, I'll pick you up at eight sharp, okay?"

I said, "Okay, see you at eight."

He got almost to the door and turned around and said, "From now on, kid, it's your ballgame. This is what you've been waiting for. But let me remind you of one thing, Big Rim is no good to us dead. He's your key to freedom."

I said, "So that's what has been bugging you. Well, you don't have to worry, I'll treat him just like a father. I want the warden's daughter to see that son of a bitch alive. And if it doesn't work, so what, I had fun catching the bastard. I can't wait to see the expression on his face when he sees me."

Tim said, "Okay, see you at eight." Then he left.

I picked up the phone and put in a person-to-person call to the warden. After about a minute or so he answered the phone.

I said, "Warden, this is Freddie."

I thought for once he was coming through the phone.

He said, "Freddie, what in the hell do you think you are doing calling me? We had a deal. You are not to call me at any time. Where in the hell is Tim Duncan?"

I said, "Look, I know what the deal was, now you just listen, because I'm only going to tell you once." I could hear him breathing hard on the other end of the line. I said, "I located Big Rim. Tim and I are bringing him in tonight. We should be there no later than nine o'clock, that's if everything goes like we got it planned. Now this is what I want you to do. You make sure we don't have any trouble coming in at the check point, because if we blow it we won't get a second chance. I want you to make sure Emily is in her bedroom in bed. Have my uniform there. Also have one there for Big Rim. Leave only the night light on in Emily's room, I'll explain the rest when I get there. See you at nine o'clock."

He was trying to say something when I hung up the phone. I didn't want to talk to him any longer. I didn't want him to mess up what I had planned. I dialed my own number, got a busy signal and left the phone off the hook. I didn't want him calling. I knew Tim had told him where I was staying. I didn't even want Toni calling either. Somehow I felt I had seen the last of her.

I kicked my shoes off and lay down across the bed. Now for the long wait. I closed my eyes, thinking about the good time Toni and I had.

At seven o'clock I was up packing my things. At seven-thirty I couldn't wait any longer. Tim would just have to pick me up there.

I got in my car and headed for the Gig's Motel.

I said, "What the hell, they can pick up the Goddamn car up there." I wanted to sit on Big Rim and make sure he didn't get out of there. I pulled up just ouside the motel. Then I decided I had better call Tim and let him know where I was. I didn't have to, he was already parked outside the motel, too. I got out of my car and walked over to his and opened the door and got in.

I said, "You were supposed to come get me."

He said, "Well, I just wanted to make sure he didn't leave. By the way, what in the hell are you doing here? I was supposed to pick you up, remember."

We both started laughing. He knew why I was there. He reached in the back seat and got a bottle of Scotch.

He said, "Might as well get you one now, who knows, you may not get another one in a long time. They don't have this kind at the Giant."

I said, "I don't see a damn thing funny about that."

I took the bottle and turned it up and took a long pull. He took the bottle and took a long pull. We both sat there looking at the watch every two minutes.

Finally, Tim said, "What the hell are we waiting for, let's wrap this case up? We can kill some time going over there."

We both got out of the car.

Tim said, "What side do you want?"

I said, "I'll take the right."

Tim said, "Here goes nothing."

I said, "Well, let's make something out of it."

When we reached the door, Tim whispered, "Okay, kid, it's your show."

I got in front of the door and took my foot and let it have it. Big Rim was lying on the couch. Before he could get on his feet I had the gun about three inches from his nose. Tim made a dash through to the other rooms.

I said, "Sit back real easy. One bad move, and you're a dead man."

Tim came back and said, "All clear."

I said, "Keep him covered."

I ran my hand under the pillow and took out Big Rim's gun. I stuck it in my belt and slapped the cuffs on him. Tim put his gun away and shoved Big Rim's shoes on his feet. Suddenly it came to him who I was.

He said, "Frankie, what in the hell are you doing here? You're supposed to be—"

I finished it for him. I said, "Sitting out in that Goddamn hole. Something changed, Big Rim."

He said, "She don't remember—or, I mean, I don't know what in the hell you are doing here."

I said, "I'll spell it out to you on the way back over to the Giant. So come on, somebody wants to see you real bad."

He said, "How in the hell did you get out? Look, Frankie, I'll make a deal with you. I got some money coming tomorrow, eight thousand. You can have half of it. You can go to Mexico. No one will ever find you."

I said, "That's nice of you, Big Rim, but on the other hand, I think I'd rather go back to the Giant."

He said, "You know this is kidnapping. You can't get away with it. You will spend the rest of your life in the Giant for this."

I said, "No more than spending the rest of my life in there for something I didn't do." I said, "You almost got away with it, Big Rim. Tomorrow at this time you were planning to be in Mexico yourself. And just think, I would still be sweating it out in that Goddamn hole called the corner pocket, all because you raped the warden's daughter and pinned the rap on me.

"I watched you make guys walk the line and sweat for eight years. But between here and the Giant, you're going to sweat much more than that. And I think I am going to enjoy it. You're going back to the Giant and help me prove I didn't rape the warden's daughter."

I looked at Tim and said, "Come on; we've wasted enough time."

Big Rim said, "You'll be spotted—I'll scream."

I said, "And if you do, I'm going to squeeze off just one

round, right through your fat head, because I don't have anything to lose. Now, come on, move. I can't wait any longer."

I caught him by the arm and gave him a shove out the door.

When we got to the car, Tim got in the front seat and I shoved Big Rim in the back seat and got in beside him. Tim brought the car to life and we were off to the Giant. Big Rim was still trying to deal.

Tim said, "Hey, Freddie, how about putting your foot in his mouth? It's okay with me."

Big Rim stopped talking.

Two quick turns and we were heading over the overpass through which the Giant was only ten miles farther.

Nobody was saying a word for a long time.

Finally Tim said, "The only problem we got is getting past the check point."

I said, "That's supposed to be taken care of, and if it's not, we just have to figure some other way to get in there—and I don't give a damn how, even if we have to ram it—so long as we get this son of a bitch to the warden's house." I looked at Big Rim and said, "Don't worry, buddy, you're going to the warden's house, if I have to drag you. No one is going to fuck this chance up. I waited too long."

I looked over at the speedometer. Tim was only doing fifty-five.

I said, "Won't this damn thing go any faster?"

Tim said, "Sure, all we have to do is get stopped, and the deal sure enough will be blown up. Come on, settle down, we've gone too far to blow it on account of speeding."

We finally made it to the turn leading to the Giant. Big Rim raised up in the seat and started looking around. I knew he was trying to spot a cop car. Just before we reached the corner, Big Rim got his wish. The cop was parked in the back of the service station on the left. Big Rim was up on the edge of the seat.

Tim said, "Keep that son of a bitch down."

I shoved Big Rim back down in the seat. Just as we got to the corner, a white Mustang rounded the corner on two wheels. He didn't see the cop car coming by him from the opposite direction. He went right across in front of Tim. Tim hit the brakes to keep from hitting him. The cop kicked on his red lights and came out of the station. He went past us after the

Mustang. I told Big Rim he could sit up now. The kid in the Mustang had blown his chance.

About that time we were at the lane leading to the check point.

Tim said, "Check point coming up."

Tim and I knew he had to roll down the window. I took a look at Big Rim. He was all eyes.

Suddenly I spotted Lieutenant Bateman. I told Tim he could let go of his breath, that the guy at the check point was in from the go.

Tim blew out wind for a long time, then he said, "Man, I sure wish you would tell me these things in the beginning."

When we reached the check point, Tim stopped.

Lieutenant Bateman looked in and said, "Okay, go on."

Tim hit the gas. I looked back and the guard was trying to tell Lieutenant Bateman something and pointing toward the car.

Tim said, "Man, did you know we were supposed to get through that easy?"

I said, "I kind of thought we would. When you left the motel I called the warden. He knew we were coming."

Just before we reached the warden's house, the lights went out on both inside and outside. Tim drove on in the driveway and stopped. We got out and both took Big Rim by the arms and led him up to the warden's door. Just as I drew my hand back to knock, the door opened. Captain Bennett said, "Come on in."

Big Rim said, "Captain, what in the hell is going on? Did you know this bastard was out? He and this fellow came to my house and kidnapped me. Where in the hell is the warden?"

Captain Bennett said, "Just take it easy, Lieutenant Bassey, we all are going to sit down and talk this thing out."

I said, "Talk, hell, we are—"

Captain Bennett said, "Now, you just hold on, I got some other business with you."

He told Tim to take the cuffs off Big Rim. While the cuffs were being removed, Captain Bennett escorted me across the room and into the dining room. I walked around looking for the warden. The room was full. I spotted the warden. He walked over to me and said, "Here put these on." He gave me my prison uniform. I looked back and Tim was behind me. He reached inside my coat and took out my gun and Big Rim's gun, too. The warden beckoned for two guards who were standing at the back door. The warden said, "Take him in and have him change clothes."

Everything was going strange. I stopped to say something to the warden, but the two guards pushed me on into the room. I began to get a little worried. I began to wonder what in the hell had gone wrong. The guards stood on opposite sides of the door. I started changing my clothes.

I said, "Where is the warden's daughter?" Neither one said a word. I said, "Are you guys surprised to see me back?" Still not a word.

I finished changing my clothes and started for the door. The two guards stopped me.

I said, "Take your hands off me. I want to see the warden. Look I'm supposed to—" I didn't finish. I heard the warden's daughter screaming. She was calling for me to come help her. I reached down and got a chair and started for the guards. The one on the left pulled the door open. They both stepped back. I rushed through the door with the chair in my hands. I was heading for the warden's daughter's room. She was still screaming. I dropped the chair when I got to her room. I looked in and she was fighting Big Rim like hell. She saw me and ran and caught me around the neck and kept saying over and over, "You wouldn't help me, Frankie, you wouldn't help me. Mr. Bassey raped me. Frankie he raped me."

I said, "Don't try to talk. Everything is going to be all right."

Her mother came and got her. She kept saying, "Mother, he raped me. Mr. Bassey raped me, mother."

Mrs. Bolden led her out of the room and into another one. When she opened the door, I had a chance to look a few of the women in the eye. They just lowered their heads. I looked around and two deputies were taking Big Rim out of the house. He was in handcuffs.

I said, "So long, you miserable son of a bitch. I hope they hang you by your balls."

Captain Bennett and Captain Roundside walked over to where I was standing.

Captain Bennett said, "I'm sorry, Frankie, or Freddie, that is."

I said, "For what, that I wasn't your man? Will you do me a favor, captain, and have some of your yard dogs take me to my cell. I am not afraid of them beating me up now, being that they know that I wasn't the one who raped the warden's daughter."

Captain Roundside said, "Not so fast. I think the warden wants to talk to you."

Tim walked over and said, "Well, Freddie, it's all over. You won. And we didn't have to shoot it out. At least I didn't have to shoot you."

I said, "It could have gone the other way, you know."

He said, "Not for a moment. You see, Freddie, you only had blanks in your gun."

He took the gun from his waist and opened the cylinder and dumped the blanks out in his hand.

I said, "Why you no good son of a bitch. You should be locked up, too. You were going to murder me without a chance."

He said, "No, you would just have been another convict killed trying to escape. And, by the way, I'll take my dough."

I took the money out of my front pocket and jammed it in his hand.

I said, "You dirty bastard, you earned it. I hope you choke on it. You want to count it?"

He said, "Naw, I trust you."

Boy, I was mad as hell.

The warden walked up and said, "Good job, Freddie."

I said, "You were in on it from the go. You set me up. You're no better than that son of a bitch there." I was pointing toward Tim. "Now you come and tell me thanks. Thanks for what, not getting my damn head blown off? How about letting me out of here before I throw up."

The warden said, "I'm afraid I can't do that. You see, I have made other arrangements."

I said, "You can make all the damn arrangements you want to. Just don't include me in any of them. Somehow I got a gut feeling I shouldn't trust you anymore. Now, if you don't mind, I'll be going to my cell."

He said, "I'm releasing you in the custody of Tim Duncan for the next thirty days. After that you are on your own."

I said, "You must be kidding. He's the one you had set up to kill me. Now you tell me you're putting me in his custody? You still ain't satisfied that I didn't rape your daughter? Why don't you just send me back to the corner pocket until my few days are up. I'll be okay. In fact, I think I would rather have that than go with him. The judge said I only had thirty days to go and that's been over two weeks now."

He said, "I'm afraid you don't have any choice, so get in there and change your clothes."

I was about to say something when the two guards took an arm apiece and led me into the room.

After I changed clothes, I came back into the room.

The warden said, "I know you have about two hundred bucks on the books, but take this. It's around two thousand. That will help you get on your feet."

I said, looking around at Tim, "If I live long enough."

The warden said, "Now, you two get the hell out of here. I've got other things to take care of."

He shook hands with Tim and we left. When we got outside, we got in Tim's car and headed out. We reached the check point where Lieutenant Bateman was. He held out his hand and said, "Good luck, Freddie." I said, "Thanks, Lieutenant Bateman, I'll need it." Tim hit the gas and we were off. I looked over my shoulder at the old place that I had called home for over eight years. I didn't like the deal at all, but it felt good leaving that place.

Just outside the prison on the main drag was the Gold Dust Motor Inn Lodge. Tim pulled over into it.

I said, "What the hell are we stopping here for?"

He said, "This is where we part company."

I said, "What the hell do you mean? How am I going to get out of this desert? What about the deal you made with the warden? You mean you're going to dump me out here in the middle of nowhere? What am I going to do for transportation?"

He reached in his pocket and took out the money I gave him. He said, "Here, you had one chance to spend it, now you're getting another one." He reached in his inside coat pocket and took out another envelope. He said, "Here, there's two thousand of the ten thousand I got for the job. Go on, take it, you earned it. That should put you up about nine thousand strong."

I took the money.

I said, "Now, will you tell me just how in the hell am I supposed to get off this damn desert?"

He handed me a card and said, "Now, when you get there, call this number. Tell the guy who you are and give him my name. He will see to it that you get work. You got it?"

I said, "Yes, I got it, but you haven't told me just how in the hell I am supposed to get there."

He said, "Oh, yes, that part. Look over your left shoulder."

I turned around and there stood Toni standing by the car the warden had let me drive. I couldn't believe it. I looked around at Tim.

He said, "Yes, the car, too. And she goes with the deal. Now that's my first order. The next one is, when you get to Frisco, you marry her. I'll be taking my vacation in about sixty days from now. I'll be expecting an invitation to dinner from both of you."

I said, in a low voice, almost a whisper, "You got it."

We both walked over to where Toni was. I gave her a long kiss.

I said to Tim, "Look, I'm sorry for the names I called you."

Tim said, "Don't be, I'm those and more."

We both laughed.

He said, "Well, I guess I'll be moving on."

He hugged Toni and gave her a kiss.

He said, "Now, if this guy doesn't behave, you get in touch with me."

She said, "I will—and Tim—thanks for everything."

Tim just walked over to his car, got in and drove off.

I caught Toni in my arms and gave her a bigger kiss than the first one.

I said, "How did you know where to come?"

She said, "Tim told me. He also told me about the deal he and the warden made night before last, about if Emily came around, and how it all depended on her. So he told me where to wait, and Freddie, I prayed many a time standing here. So here I am. Anymore questions?"

I said, "No more. Let's get the hell out of here."

We got in the car and started off.

I said, "Just to think of all the names I called that guy. He didn't have to split his money with me. It was all his."

I looked over to my left. I could see the warden's house in full view. I slowed down to get another good look at the prison.

I knew about that time of night Leo was putting some bad blues down, and the guys were all taking it in. I said, "I never thought things would come out this way. And you see right over there behind that clump of trees, that's the warden's house. That's where it all started. And out of all of it, I got my freedom and you. And none of it would have ever happened if it hadn't been for the warden's daughter."

Foreword to Small Town Robberies

Leo Servettie spent almost fifteen years in the federal prison in Kansas. He had gone there for bank robbery. The F.B.I. had put a close net around Leo since he had been out. But Leo slipped through the circle. He picked up his gang that he had put together while in prison and headed south, to go into bank robbery again. But this time, in a different way.

After two good jobs that netted him almost seventy-five thousand dollars, Leo made one mistake.

The stolen boat ran upon the bank of the Mississippi River on the Tennessee side, giving the F.B.I. one shot to start from. And with that one shot, Leo went back to prison and two of his men went down Shady Lane. That broke up Leo's gang and there were no more *small town robberies.*

Small Town Robberies

It was early in April. Spring had just begun to peek through. Winter visitors had just about all returned to the North. All the small towns in Southeast Missouri were getting ready for farming. Banks had begun to get in more money in order to help out farmers and small businesses for the coming summer. No one expected that what happened could, and why? Leo Serettie had gotten released from the federal prison in Kansas where he had been serving time for a bank robbery some fifteen years ago.

Leo was living in St. Louis, Missouri, and was being closely watched. But somehow he had slipped from under the closely guarded circle around him.

It was about four-twenty-one evening when the F.B.I. received a call from the little town of Portersville, Missouri. The bank had been robbed of some twenty-eight thousand dollars. The police chief , John Bonn, had nothing to go on but three abandoned autos, and a case to offer the F.B.I. that would not be solved overnight.

Police Chief, John Bonn, was sitting in his office when two men walked in and presented themselves as two detectives from upstate New York with a warrant for a man they had heard was living in this small town. After assuring them that he had not seen the man, they were off. That was the first part of Leo's set-up. To find out how many were working at the police station. The rest of Leo's gang was George Holley and Guy Foley, the two who passed as detectives from out of state, Britt Jackson, who was black and a decoy man, and Ed Fry, who worked along with Leo.

Britt Jackson had gone to the only pool hall in town, over on Central Avenue. After playing several games of pool and losing , he decided not to pay up. After a heated argument with the owner, Britt knocked the owner down, drew his gun and fired two shots at him. Missing, of course, he then ran to the door and fired two more shots at him as he ran to the pick-up he had stolen earlier. Meanwhile, Leo and Ed were sizing up the bank.

George Holley and Guy Foley had gone back into the station after they heard the police cars racing to the pool hall. George grabbed the switchboard operator and put his gun to his head and shoved him over to the door where Guy was. Guy then shoved the door to the chief's office open, rushed over, gun in his hand, and tied Chief John Bonn and the switchboard operator together and put them on the floor. At that time George ripped the phone loose, while Guy gagged Chief Bonn and the operator.

Meanwhile Ed and Leo were scooping money from the

shelves in the bank's vault, while everyone else was lying flat on the floor.

Britt Jackson had made his way to the plane they had landed just outside of town at an old abandoned airstrip. Ed had given him instructions on how to start the engine. About three minutes later, George and Guy had arrived at the plane. After about five minutes more, Leo and Ed arrived. They all loaded up and were off in the air, leaving behind three stolen autos.

After getting information on the man who shot up the pool hall, Officer Roy Silver went to his patrol car and tried desperately to contact his headquarters. After about three minutes went by, he told Patrolman Lee String he was going by the station to see why he couldn't make contact.

Officer Silver walked into the station, didn't see the operator, and headed to Chief Bonn's office. What he saw he didn't want to believe. The chief and the operator were tied together and the bank alarm was blasting like crazy. He reached down and untied the chief and the operator. Then he reached under and shut off the bank alarm. Chief Bonn scrambled to his feet and told Officer Silver to come with him to the bank. Then he turned to the operator and told him to get in touch with Captain Wertz at the highway patrol station. "Tell him to come meet me at the bank." As they headed out, Chief Bonn radioed for Patrolman Jim Davis to meet him at the bank. After arriving at the bank, he found the bank's president white as a sheet. In nothing flat Captain Wertz arrived. After getting what information he could, he and Captain Wertz headed back to his office.

Once inside, he yelled to the switchboard operator to call in every off-duty patrolman he had. Then he headed for his office, beckoning for Captain Wertz. He sat down and offered Captain Wertz a chair.

He looked at Captain Wertz and said, "Mike, you are not going to believe what I am about to tell you."

Captain Wertz spoke for the first time, "Try me."

Chief Bonn leaned across the desk, folded his hands and began telling Captain Wertz what had happened.

After he finished, Captain Wertz said, "John, you had best

get in touch with the F.B.I. This looks like something big and well organized. I don't think that it's anyone local."

After assuring Captain Wertz that he was right, the operator opened the door.

He said, "Captain, your men have found two autos and one pickup truck, one answering the description of the car that was used in the bank holdup, the pickup answering the description of the one that was at the shooting at the pool hall."

He told the operator to tell them to stand by, he and Chief Bonn were on their way. "Meanwhile, get hold of the F.B.I. and have them meet me at the airstrip."

After receiving the call, Inspector Dalton and Agent Ross were assigned to the case. Chief Bonn and Captain Wertz, along with a few other patrolmen, waited at the old, abandoned airstrip. It wasn't long before Inspector Dalton and Agent Ross landed in a helicopter. After introducing themselves, they all started going over the autos. Finding no fingerprints, they decided to go back into town to Chief Bonn's office. Captain Wertz told one of his men to stand by until they got a tow truck out to pick up the autos. They all got into Chief Bonn's car and headed for town. They stopped by the bank. After getting more information from Mr. Wise, the bank president, they headed for Chief Bonn's office. On the way Captain Wertz mentioned the shooting at the pool hall. Inspector Dalton decided they had better stop by there first. He was sure there was a connection between the two.

After getting the information that Britt Jackson was not a local, they headed to Chief Bonn's office. Once inside, Inspector Dalton notified all airstrips to be on the lookout for a small two-engine plane carrying five people. He looked at Chief Bonn and Captain Wertz and said, "We'll just have to wait until something breaks." Meanwhile Leo and his gang had landed in a deserted area along the Mississippi River on the Tennessee side.

The next town they were plannint to hit was a little town on the Mississippi River called Caruthersville, Missouri. Leo, who had bootlegged whisky all through these parts of Missouri, knew all about these little towns, and knew the surrounding area like a book.

Now that they had landed, they needed transportation from

the plane across the river. That Leo had already figured out. It was up to Britt to get them transportation from the plane. Britt changed into some old overalls. Leo handed him a shotgun. He was to pose as a hunter in making his way five miles to a service station and eating place. There he was to lay out until dark, steal a car, and head back to the plane. After getting last minute instructions from Leo, Britt headed out.

Then Leo opened up the sack and they started counting the money. It came to $28,457.89.

Ed turned to Leo and said, "Are you going to split even with Britt?"

Leo didn't take kindly to being asked that. He gave every man a moment's stare. Then he spoke.

"When we started out we promised to give every man an equal share." Ed started to say something, but Leo cut him off. "Ed, you just shut up and listen. That's the way we started out and that's the way it's going to be, and the first man tries to beat the other one I will personally blow his brains out. Now, is that clear?"

They knew Leo meant every word.

"One more job and we split, and I mean down to the penny. Once we make it back to St. Louis, every man will go his own way. Lay low for six months, then we meet and head for another state."

George asked, "What about spending the money, won't it be too hot?"

Leo said, "That's a good question. After we split, I'll buy back five grand from each one of you. That will hold you until we meet again in six months. So don't go spending any of the hot money. Keep it separate from the rest. . .and make sure you get the hell out of St. Louis. Go to Chicago, Detroit, upstate New York, anywhere."

They all got quiet when they heard the noise of an automobile.

Leo looked at his watch and said, "I'm not looking for Britt for another fifteen minutes."

Everyone laid low while the auto came closer. The auto stopped and after about ten seconds the horn sounded, two long and two short. They all yelled, "Britt! He made it!" They all climbed down and headed for the car. They were all greeting

Britt while Leo pointed the way. They headed up the river to an old shack where they took care of boats for fishermen. The owner was gone, and it didn't take George long to pick the lock on a boat. They loaded in and headed for the Missouri side of the Mississippi River.

Leo knew that the police would be looking for them in a car, so he made another move that Inspector Dalton and Agent Ross would never think he would. He and his gang had made their way back to a little place on the river called the Sea Wall. There they had abandoned the autos and headed up the river in the boat they had stolen that night. Leo was a funny fellow. He would never tell his men from day to day how he had planned everything. Just before he would get ready to make his move, he would tell the fellows what he planned to do. He said it was better—that way no one had a chance to sleep over his assignment.

The next morning about 10 o'clock, Captain Wertz contacted Inspector Dalton at the Motor Motel Inn where they had put up for the night. He told him that men from the highway patrol district in Hayti, Missouri, were blocking off Highways No. 84 and No. 61 at that point. The bank in Caruthersville, Missouri, about six miles from there, had been robbed just like the one here in Portersville. Inspector Dalton asked how far it was from where he was. Captain Wertz told him it was about fourteen miles. He told Captain Wertz to pick him up in five minutes.

Inspector Dalton and Agent Ross headed to Caruthersville, Missouri. Patrolman Ralph Jones was reporting for work that morning when he found Chief Hancock and his switchboard operator in the same position that Chief Bonn and his operator was in back at Portersville. Chief Bonn's town bank was a little bit better off than Chief Hancock's. Chief Hancock's town bank had not only lost forty thousand dollars, but also a bank guard. Officer Dick Williams was killed in the exchange of gunfire with Leo and Ed Fry. Chief Hancock had every available man he could find out looking for the thieves. About twelve noon Inspector Dalton and Agent Ross arrived at Chief Hancock's office. After introducing themselves, Chief Hancock started giving Inspector Dalton and Agent Ross what little he did have, which was nothing in the way of a good lead.

The switchboard operator opened the door and told Chief Hancock they had something. Three autos had been found by two young boys over behind the Sea Wall. One of the boys got suspicious when he saw the cars. He knew one of the cars. It belonged to his neighbor, and he remembered his neighbor telling his dad his car had been stolen. Inspector Dalton and Chief Hancock headed for the Sea Wall.

At this time Leo and his gang had come to a little town that sits off the river called Sikeston, Missouri. Ed Fry took the boat, tied the steering wheel, and headed it straight across the river. Leo and his gang headed out to a little abandoned shack just off the river. There they were to wait for Leo's next move.

Upon arriving at the Sea Wall, Inspector Dalton asked Chief Hancock if there was a boat dock anywhere around. At that time the operator called Chief Hancock and told him that they spotted the plane over on the Tennessee side of the river. Also, that the old man that took care of the boats just up the river a little ways had reported a boat being stolen, and he gave him the description of it. Inspector Dalton told him to get in touch with the Coast Guard and tell them to be on the alert for the boat.

Back at the bank a photo had been snapped, and the picture on it was Leo Servettie, known bank robber, whom the F.B.I. had put away once. After checking with the St. Louis office, Inspector Dalton learned that Leo, just two days earlier, had jumped the security they had around him. Inspector Dalton knew by now he would be trying to make it out of the state. Leo and his gang weren't only facing bank robbery, but now murder had entered the picture.

Back at the old farmhouse, light of day had just about gone. Leo was issuing plans for the next move and the call was going Britt Jackson's way again. This time George Holley was going alone. George was to pose as a farmer and buy himself a tractor and flat trailer. Britt was to be his farm boy. After they purchased the tractor, they were to go by the grain house and buy a load of hay. Together they were to drive back to the farmhouse. After Leo had given out his plans they counted up the money: $57,412.20. Eleven thousand four hundred eighty-two dollars and forty cents apiece. The money was to stay together until they were out. They all decided to bed down for the night.

Chief Hancock's office got the report from the Coast Guard that they had found the boat rammed against the bank of the Mississippi River on the Tennessee side. It was the first mistake Leo had made. The boat was supposed to crash and sink, leaving no trace of where they had gotten off to.

Where the boat was found there wasn't a town on the Tennessee side for twenty-five miles, so Inspector Dalton and Agent Ross knew it could only have come from the Missouri side. Early the next morning they headed back to Sikeston, Missouri.

George and Britt made their rounds as planned and now they were back at the farmhouse. After hauling out the center part of the haystack, Leo, George, Ed, and Guy all got inside. Britt put the final touch on the haystack, mounted the tractor and headed off to St. Louis.

As the bank opened in Sikeston, Inspector Dalton and Agent Ross were there to warn the president that Leo and his gang were somewhere in town. While they were talking, Agent Ross stepped outside the office to have a look around. Mr. Stanley Hanson who had sold the tractor and trailer that morning was there at the bank to make an early deposit. He was telling the teller how this guy just walked in, took the first tractor he showed him, and had this big colored boy take it around and latch it on to one of those flatbeds. Agent Ross walked over, showed his I.D. and asked where these guys were heading. Mr. Hanson said he didn't know. Ross asked did he know the farmer. Mr. Hanson said he had never seen the man before. Agent Ross walked back to the office and told Inspector Dalton he thought he had something. After explaining to Inspector Dalton what he had just gotten, Inspector Dalton told Captain Wertz to get in touch with the town police station and find out if any of his men had seen a tractor pulling a flat trailer. Also to have his men be on the lookout and put up road blocks and have a helicopter meet them just outside of town on Route 61.

Inspector Dalton and Agent Ross then headed back into the bank. They asked the president to let them use his phone. Dalton called Captain Wertz and told him that he had road blocks set up all around, and the one going north was set just below the weight station. Then they loaded up and went out to meet the chopper. Once aboard the chopper, they started scouting the area's back roads. After about five minutes a call came in that one of the highway patrolmen had spotted an ordinary tractor pulling a load of hay on a flatbed and going north. Inspector Dalton told him not to stop the tractor or follow it—just overtake it at the weight station. In about two minutes the chopper had the tractor in sight. Inspector Dalton told the pilot to get up high so they wouldn't think they were being followed, and to set down at the weight station. When the chopper sat down at the weight station, Agent Ross got out and went inside. It was a usual thing for a highway patrol car to be parked at the weight station, but not a chopper, so they picked up again and headed on down to the road block, which couldn't be seen from the weight station.

When the chopper was back in the air, Agent Ross and the two highway patrolmen inside the station got out of sight. Britt Jackson pulled into the station and up onto the scales. Once on the scales, the weight man told him to come inside and get his ticket. Agent Ross knew that Leo and the rest of the gang were all sealed up inside the hay, so when Britt walked inside the station, he was seized by Agent Ross and the two highway patrolemen. They put a hand over his mouth so he could not warn the others. In nothing flat they had him handcuffed and gagged. Then Agent Ross went out and mounted the tractor.

As he pulled off, Leo and the others gave a big handshake and grinned to each other.

Ed said, "St. Louis, here we come."

In about two minutes, Agent Ross stopped the tractor about ten feet from the road block.

Leo said, "What in the hell is he stopping for?"

Agent Ross jumped off the tractor and headed for cover.

At that time Inspector Dalton yelled out, "F.B.I., Leo. You and your men come out with your hands up."

Nobody moved. They were all shocked. Captain Wertz was holding a torch. He lit it and threw it on top of the haystack. Leo and the rest heard the hay burning and smelled the smoke. With gun in hand, Ed kicked out the side of the haystack. Guy leaned out to fire a shot—George did the same, but was cut down in a hail of bullets by the F.B.I. and other officers. Leo and Ed, who never showed, started yelling, "Don't shoot." They both threw out their guns and raised their hands. Inspector

Dalton told them to step down. They both did. Leo had the money sack in his hand. Once on the ground, he looked back over his shoulder at the burning hay. He quickly tossed the sack over his head into the haystack. One of the highway patrolmen very alertly grabbed his fire extinguisher and sprayed it on the fire, while Captain Wertz retrieved the money bag.

By that time the two patrolmen had arrived, with Britt handcuffed in the back seat. Leo and Ed were also handcuffed and put in the back seat along with Britt Jackson.

Guy Foley and George Holley, who chose to shoot it out, had to wait for a different ride—a ride they would never know about—in an *ambulance*.

Once again the F.B.I. proved to be ever on the alert side, going into a crime that was completely new, but as the others: it's now history.

Foreword to My Last Christmas

The story you are about to read is one of the most heart warming stories you will ever read. It's a story that has waited twelve years to be told. It's about a young black man named Tommie Foley, who was raised in a small town in southeast Missouri, right in the heart of what they call the "Boot Hills."

Tommie Foley had worked hard to get where he was and he was just about to be promoted to foreman on his job when the little world he had built up so well came tumbling down. It was the greediness for money on the part of one of his best friends, Tom Moley, and one of the town's crooked policemen, Officer Frank Bennett, that caused Tommie to lose everything he had worked and lived for. Now, after fourteen years, Tommie feels he should tell the shocking story to the world, and why he looks back to the year of 1964, and can remember it so well as the year of "My Last Christmas."

My Last Christmas

As I stood there with the chilly winter wind whipping around the tears flowing down my cheeks, somewhere far away I could hear a voice saying, "Merry Christmas and welcome home."

I knew it was God speaking to me, for my family, my wife

Ruby and my twin girls, Coleidia and Loleadia, who were buried beneath the cold ground just two feet from where I was standing. Just at the head of their graves was where my father-in-law was buried. As I looked around me, the ground was just about covered with snow. Although it had quit snowing, you could tell from the clouds above that it was coming back again, and as I stood there, my mind went back about twelve years. The Christmas of 1963. That's how long I had been gone from that little town I was raised in, a little place in southeast Missouri called Hayti, down in the boot heel of Missouri. But it was home, and we were happy there—at least I was until my life came apart—at which time I spent my last Christmas, which will stick in my mind forever and ever, because at that Christmas I lost the most wonderful things in my life, and they were about two feet from where I was standing—my wife and two kids. Looking back to that Christmas, it all unfolds before my eyes. Here is how it happened.

I was working at a little factory, the Letha Shoe Factory on the outskirts of town. I had gone to work that morning just like any other morning, hoping for my promotion to come through. I was up for a foreman position, and, boy, I could hardly wait until it came through.

That morning, around ten o'clock, Mr. Ben Leaveydon, the foreman whom I was supposed to replace, came over to my station where I was working. He took a look around, then put his arm on my shoulder and said, "Tommie, when you finish that piece you are working on, I want you to come into my office."

I said, "Sure, sir, it will only be another five or ten minutes."

He said, "Take your time."

He kind of half smiled and walked away. Boy, I just knew this was the big day, the day I had been waiting for a long time. I really began to feel good.

I finished the piece I was working on and headed to the bathroom to wash up. I wanted to look pretty good going inside to get my promotion.

However, when I got inside, it was all a different story—and what a story.

Inside the office were a few other people, some I knew and some I didn't.

Mr. Leaveydon said, "Come on in, Tommie, and have a seat."

He was seated behind the desk. Sitting on the side of his desk was the superintendent, Mr. Charles Jefferson. To my right was Mr. Benny Gilliam, president of the company. And to my left was the town's chief of police, Mr. Robert Banks. There were two other men I didn't know; in fact, I didn't remember seeing them around town before.

After I sat down, Mr. Leaveydon said, "Tommie, you know just about everybody here, except these two fellows"—pointing to the two fellows standing behind him. He said, "They have a warrant for your arrest."

I got to my feet and said, "What damn arrest? For what?"

He said, "You'd best go along with them."

I said, "Somebody is going to tell me what I am being arrested for." I turned to Chief Banks and said, "Chief, what is this all about? Don't I have a right to know?"

He said, "Yes, you have."

I said, "Well, what in hell is this all about?"

Chief Banks said, "Tommie, your car was searched just a little while ago by myself and these two men and we found this package of heroin. In your lunch bucket we found another package of heroin. Now these are the two packages that were found and I guess you don't know how they got there."

I said, "Hell, no—I made my own lunch this morning, and I know what I put in my lunch bucket. I don't know what the hell is going on here, but somebody better get their people together. I don't know a damn thing about any dope—hell, I wouldn't know the stuff if you showed it to me."

Chief Banks said, "I'm afraid you are going to have to come downtown to the station with me, Tommie." He took out his handcuffs and slapped them on my wrist and his. He said, "We can talk about it down at the station." He picked up the two bags and threw them to the two F.B.I. officers.

We left out of the office and headed right down through the factory. Everybody stopped working and looked at me being escorted out of the factory. You might have thought it was a power failure, me, Tommie Foley, who was supposed to be the next foreman, now being escorted out of the place in handcuffs. I looked from one side of the factory to the other, where whispering had already begun. I could almost read their minds and the thoughts going through them—*was he caught stealing something?*

I was well liked by ninety percent of the workers, and that ninety percent wanted to see me make foreman. It was only a few who didn't, but that few didn't matter. I had worked there for twelve years, and they knew I could handle the job.

I didn't think anybody hated me bad enough to plant dope in my car and lunch bucket, but if that was the case, somebody must have.

When we all got outside the door I saw the police towing my car away. I was put in the back seat of Chief Banks's car. One of the F.B.I. men got in beside me. All the way to the station, nobody said a word. After we reached the station, I was taken inside, fingerprinted, and had a mug shot taken. Chief Banks told the desk clerk to book me on possession of drugs.

He said, "Set the bond at the usual amount, ten thousand dollars."

The clerk said, "Tommie, do you want to call anybody?"

I said, "Later, Roy, right now I want to do some thinking."

I kept denying that I had any knowledge of what they were talking about. So they finally gave up and told the clerk to put me in one of the cells. I went to my cell. I started walking up and down the floor like a cat. After about another hour had passed, I called Roy and told him I was ready to make a phone call.

When I got Ruby, my wife, on the phone, I told her what had happened. First, I thought she was upset about what they had done to me, but I found out that that wasn't what she was so upset about. It was because the matter was going to embarrass her and the kids before her friends, and most of all—her church group. Somehow I got tired of listening to what she was saying, so I said, "Ruby, Goddammit, would you just hang up the damn phone and call Tom and have him come down here and get me out of this hell hole." Then I hung the phone up.

Roy Cook, the jailer, took me back to my cell.

He said, "Tommie, I don't believe all this stuff about you, but you understand I got to do my job."

I said, "I know, Roy, I just don't know what the hell is going on."

Tom Moley is one of my best friends. We go back to grade school together. He had a small joint on the outskirts of town where everybody went to dance, and have a little after-evening fun. While Roy and I were talking, Tom came in.

He said, "Man, what in the hell are you doing in jail? This ain't like you. I couldn't believe it when Ruby called me. What in the hell are you in for?"

I said, "Would you believe dope for a start?"

Tom said, "Dope? You got to be kidding."

I said, "Ask Roy."

Roy had already overheard us talking and when Tom looked around, Roy just bowed his head. Tom asked what was my bond. I told him it was ten thousand dollars.

He said, "Ten grand! Man, you don't get a bond set that high when you kill a cop." He looked at Roy and said, "No offense, Roy." Tom said, "I got to see the chief, because I have to sign some property over to get you out."

I said, "Man, I don't care what you do, just get me out of this place. I got to get in touch with Alex Brandon."

Mr. Alex Brandon was one of the best lawyers in that neck of the woods. After Tom went and talked with Chief Banks he came back. He looked at me and said, "OK, Tommie, let's get the hell out of here. We got to get in touch with Alex."

We left the station and headed straight for Mr. Brandon's office.

I said, "Tom, I don't know what the hell is going on, but somebody is going to come up with some straight answers."

We got in the car and headed for Mr. Brandon's office. His door was standing open. We didn't stop at the desk, even though the girl was sitting there. We walked right into Mr. Brandon's office and sat down.

He said, "OK, Tommie, what you say we get right to the point."

I said, "Alex, somebody planted some dope in my car and lunch bucket. The F.B.I. came by and searched the car and found it. From what Mr. Leaveydon says, they also came inside and checked my lunch bucket. Now how it got there is far beyond me. But here I am charged with selling it, and most of all, I was escorted from the factory, right down in front of everybody."

Mr. Brandon asked was I there when they searched my car.

I said, "Hell, no."

He said, "What about the lunch bucket?"

I said, "I wasn't there either. When I knew anything about how they had come by it, I was in Mr. Leaveydon's office. They had it all laid out, and told me where they got it from. Chief Banks said he was with the two F.B.I. men when they found it, and as we were leaving for the slammer, they were towing my car away—and would you believe the bastards still got my two ham sandwiches I brought for my lunch."

Mr. Brandon and Tom laughed.

Mr. Brandon said, "Well, there is nothing I can do today—give me a day or two. I don't think you have much to worry about. Meanwhile, you stay home, and if there is anything you forgot to tell me, don't hesitate to call me, OK?"

I said, "OK, but right now that means I'm out of work."

He said, "Have you done your Christmas shopping yet?"

I said we were planning to go tomorrow.

He said, "Have you got any money in the bank?"

I said, "What little Ruby and I have saved over the few years."

He said, "First thing in the morning I want you to go over to the bank and draw out all you have, because if you don't, they are going to tie it up. See you in a day or two."

Tom and I got up and left.

On the way home Tom said, "Man, who would plant some stuff on you, and why?"

I said, "So far my mind is blank. I know there are a few fellows in the factory who don't want to see me make foreman, but I don't think they would go this far."

Tom said, "Man, you would be surprised just how far they would go to keep a black man down."

When we reached my house, Tom said, "Well, I got to get back to the joint. If you need any wheels, you can use my pickup. Meanwhile, I will be by and take you to the bank in the morning."

I said, "Thanks again, Tom. I'll make it up to you."

He said, "Forget it, that's what friends are for." Then he took off.

So far didn't nothing make any sense. The whole God-damn thing was crazy.

I slowly walked to the porch, looked around, and then went in. Ruby was in the kitchen seated at the table. I went around behind her to give her the usual kiss, but before I reached her, she got up and walked the other way.

I said, "What the hell is wrong with you? I lose my job, get locked up, charged with selling dope, and then I come home and get the cold shoulder from you. You act like I am guilty of all the stuff. This ain't no time to play crazy. How the hell do you think I felt?"

She said, "It is all over town. Everybody is calling. I am so embarrassed I don't know what to do."

I said, "You think I'm happy? Ruby, we are supposed to be man and wife, stick by each other through thick and thin. Now here I am needing you, and you turn the other way. What kind of woman are you? You haven't asked me one time is it true. You are more concerned about your damned church group and what they think."

She said, "Stop shouting, the kids will hear you."

I said, "Ah, what is the use in trying to talk to you."

I walked out of the kitchen and went into the girls' room. They were watching TV. They stopped watching TV and came over and gave me my usual hug and kiss. That was the best comfort I had had all day. I told them I would see them at dinner. "Meanwhile, don't forget your school work."

I went out into the other room just in time to catch Ruby leaving.

I said, "Where are you going? You haven't even fixed dinner."

She said, "You can heat yours and the girls' TV dinners. I am late for a church meeting."

I said, "Couldn't you put that off just this one time?"

She said, "They are expecting me."

I said, "I am expecting you to stay home and be with me, too. I lose my job, and all these other things, and all you can think about is some Goddamned meeting. Go on, get the hell out of here, I'll be better off with you out of the house anyway."

I stepped aside and let her out. Then I went over and sank down in the lounge chair. I said to myself, "What in the hell is going on?" I couldn't think straight. I must have sat there better than an hour. Coleidia and Loleadia came in and one said, "Daddy, when are we going to eat?" The other one asked where was Mom. Being that I couldn't tell one from the other, I said, "Make you guys a deal. Mother had to go to church for a meeting. Now if you guys will light the oven and then dig out some TV dinners, I'll fix them. Is it a deal?"

They said yes and made a dash for the kitchen. Being twelve years of age they could have fixed dinner. Ruby had taught them how to cook when they were ten.

I said, "Don't worry about mother, she will probably eat out with the group."

I went in and fixed the TV dinners. Then we sat down and ate. After we finished, we went in and watched TV until around eight-thirty. I said, "OK you two, bed time. Go get your showers and hit the sack." They both were off and heading for the shower.

After the girls had gone to bed, I called Tom.

I said, "Tom, what do you make of this mess?"

He said, "Tommie, my wife and I were just talking about you. We can't make head nor tail of it. It's something wrong somewhere." He said, "Where is Ruby? Betty wants to talk to her."

I said, "She left around six o'clock. She had a meeting to go to."

He said, "At a time like this?"

I said, "I know, Tom. I couldn't understand it myself. She has been acting a little strange lately. Well, thanks for the chat—see you in the morning."

He said, "In the morning" and hung up.

I went in, took a shower and lay down across the bed. I must have dozed off to sleep. I rolled over and looked for Ruby and she wasn't there. I looked at the clock—it was half past one. I got up and looked in the girls' room. I still didn't see her and began to get worried. I made a few phone calls to some of her church members. They all said the same thing. The church meeting broke up at ten thirty. I sat there on the side of the bed wondering what had happened to her. Suddenly I heard a car pull up. At least that is what I thought. I pulled the curtain back just in time to see the car pulling off. I didn't recognize the car. Ruby was almost in the front door. Just as she put her key in the hole I opened the door.

I said, "Where in the world have you been?"

She said, "We have a new member from out of town. She brought me home and we set out there in front of the house talking." She said, "Now, are you accusing me of cheating?"

I said, "Hell no, I was just worried about you. Let's forget it, OK?"

She walked into the bedroom with me right behind her. I sat on the side of the bed.

I said, "Ruby, what is happening to us? Maybe I am just upset over what happened today. That is a lot for a man to go through."

She said, "Tommie, can't it wait until tomorrow?"

I got mad. I said, "Sure, sure, it can wait until tomorrow, and if not tomorrow, maybe the next day, and if not then, maybe some time next week. What the hell am I trying to tell you for? You're only my wife."

I gave up and took one of the pillows off the bed and got some cover from the closet and went into the living room. I made me a bed on the courch and went to sleep.

When I woke up the next morning, nobody was in the house but me. I looked at the clock and it was just a little past nine o'clock. I knew the bank opened at nine thirty. I dressed and called Tom. Betty said he was already on his way. I said thanks and hung up. I no more than had hung up the phone when Tom blew his horn. I went out and got in the car and we headed to town. It didn't take us any time to get to the bank. I got out and went inside. The line had just begun to form. I was the second one in line.

When the teller finally got to me, she said, "Mr. Foley, can I help you?"

I said, "Yes, I want to close my account."

She said, "All of it?"

I said, "Every nickel."

She said, "You have twenty-three dollars and twenty-four

cents in interest, bringing your total to two thousand eight hundred and sixty-nine dollars and forty cents. Does that sound right?"

I said, "You are right on the nose."

She said, "How do you want it?"

I said, "Give me twenty-five hundred in one-hundred-dollar-bills, and the rest in tens and twenties."

She counted out the money and I recounted it. She gave me some rubber bands and I was off and heading out the door. Just as I was about to get back in the car, I spotted the two F.B.I. men, who were with Chief Banks. I told Tom that they were the two guys that were supposed to have found the dope in my car. I think we had gotten there just in time, because when they came out of the bank, the one that had the piece of paper in his hand seemed quite unhappy. He took the paper and threw it in the car. They didn't see Tom and me. Tom started the motor and left.

I took the hundreds and gave them to Tom. I said, "You hold on to them for me until I get this mess straightened out, and if I don't, you see to it that Ruby and the kids get it—OK? I'm going to use the rest of this to get the girls' Christmas gifts—and, by the way, I want to use your pickup."

He said, "You got it."

We headed out to Tom's house. I took the pickup and told him I would call later. I headed right back to town. I stopped by the station to see Chief Banks. Roy told me he had just left.

I said, "Well, I'm going to do some shopping for the girls. Tell Chief Banks I'll stop by later this evening."

Then I left. I pulled out and headed up town and, for the rest of the day, I went Christmas shopping. I finally finished up and headed home.

I pulled into the driveway, got out and went around to the back of the truck and got an armful of boxes. Just as I was about to ring the doorbell, the door opened. I couldn't see who opened the door, I just said thanks and stepped inside. Before I could make the next step I was hit over the head with something hard and tripped, all at the same time. That is when the lights went out. The next thing I knew, somebody was pouring cold water on my face. I shook my head and tried to get up. That's when

I found out my hands were tied behind my back. I heard a man's voice say, "Sit him up." I couldn't make out the faces because they had stockings over their heads.

One said, "OK, Tommie, what did you do with the rest of the stuff?"

I said, "What stuff are you talking about? I don't know anything about any damn stuff."

He said, "Now, Tommie, don't play crazy. We know you got the rest of it somewhere, and you are going to tell us where it is, now, aren't you?"

I said, "Whatever you fellows want, I don't have it. That stuff they found in my car and lunch box was planted there. Now if it is the money you want, you can have it. It's about two hundred bucks in my front pocket. Take it and get the hell out of here."

He said, "The stuff you're holding out is worth two hundred thousand. Now why should we take a lousy two hundred bucks?"

That is when they began to work me over until I passed out.

I woke up under the water treatment again.

Then they were going over the same questions again. I finally told them they were wasting their time.

"You fellows can beat me all night and I still can't tell you any more than I already have."

The one that was doing the heavy work said, "If you want to see your wife again, you better start giving some better answers."

I said, "Ruby! What have you done with my wife?"

Nobody said a word.

I knew the kids would be coming home anytime now. I said, in a whisper, "Oh, God, don't let them hurt my kids."

One said, "Tommie, you got twenty-four hours to come up with some better answers, and if you don't make good, remember, you were the one who failed your wife."

They both left out the front door. I rolled over on the floor and tried to get my hands loose. They were tied too tight, so I settled down and waited for the girls to get home. I said to myself, "This is the one time I hope they don't decide to stop off and play."

I don't know how long I lay there waiting, but it seemed like forever. Finally I heard the girls' voices. When they saw me on the floor they both began to cry.

I said, "Come on, you guys, don't cry. One of you cut me loose."

Coleidia was the one who went and got the knife. When she came back into the room, she said, "Daddy, there is a man lying on the kitchen floor, and, daddy, he ain't moving either."

I said, "Come on, cut daddy loose."

She finally cut me loose. I made a beeline for the kitchen. I took a look at who it was and couldn't believe what I saw. It was Willie Wright. He was dead. I told the girls to go to their room. They didn't argue. I got on the phone and called Chief Banks.

I said, "Chief Banks, you better come over to my house right away. Something has happened you should know about."

He said, "What is wrong, Tommie?"

I said, "Willie Wright is here on my kitchen floor, dead."

Chief Banks didn't say a word—he just hung up his phone. Then I got on the phone and called Tom. I told him what had happened.

He said, "Give me about twenty minutes, okay?"

Just as I hung up the phone, Chief Banks and Frank Miles were at the door. I opened it and let them in. I pointed toward the kitchen. Chief Banks reached down and felt Willie's neck.

He said, "He is dead all right."

He told Frank to call an ambulance and have somebody come out from the lab.

He looked around the place and said, "My God, Tommie, what the hell went through here? And what the hell happened to you? Maybe you had better start from the beginning."

I said, "Maybe we better sit down, too."

I said, "Chief, I'll tell you like this. Ever since you came and got me off the job, things have been happening. I went to the bank this morning and drew out my life savings."

He said, "I know about that. That worried me. Are you planning on skipping town?"

I said, "Not on your life. I drew my money out on my lawyer's advice. If I didn't, the Feds would have tied it up."

He said, "I know that also. They were pretty mad that you beat them to it. Now back to all this going on here."

I said, "After I drew out the money, Tom carried me out to his house so I could pick up his truck, being that you guys took my car and didn't give a damn how I got around. Well, I got the truck and headed back to town to do some shopping for the girls for Christmas. I called Ruby at home and no one answered the phone so I went shopping by myself; that you can check on in town. I came home and took an armload of gifts and started for the door. I couldn't see anybody when the door opened for me. I took another step inside and that's when the lights went out. When I came to, with the help of a bucket of water, my hands were tied behind my back. Two guys were standing over me with stocking masks over their faces. They wanted to know what I did with the rest of their stuff. I told them I didn't know anything about what they were talking about, so they worked me over some more. After a few minutes they told me if I wanted to see my wife again, I would come up with their stuff. They gave me twenty-four hours. Then they left. The kids came home and cut me loose. When one of them went for the knife, she came back and told me that there was a man laying on the kitchen floor. When I came in to check, that is what I found—then I got on the phone and called you. After I talked to you I called Tom. He was supposed to have been here—and that's just about it."

About that time Frank came back into the kitchen. He was looking around Willie's body when he said, "Hey, look what I found." He fumbled in his pocket and took out his pencil and ran it down the barrel of the gun.

I said, "Hey, that's my gun."

Chief Banks moved Willie's head to one side. Willie had been shot once right behind the left ear. He told Frank to hold the gun for the lab. Just about that time the ambulance came. They loaded Willie's body up and left. Then the lab men came.

I said, "Chief, what about my wife?"

He said, "I have someone checking on it."

I said, "To hell with checking. I want my wife back. These guys gave me twenty-four hours to come up with their stuff."

He said, "What damn stuff? I keep hearing you mention stuff. What Goddamn stuff are you talking about?"

I said, "I wish to hell I knew, chief. I guess they mean that dope they put in my car. I don't know what damn stuff. These guys were the ones who put that shit in my lunch bucket and car."

He said, "Take it easy, Tommie. I admit something came up this morning. We found out that there was a dope shipment headed to Memphis and Hayti was supposed to be a relay town."

I said, "Well, if you think I had anything to do with it here, you are wrong. I wasn't the relay man"

He said, "Some was found in your possession."

I said, "Well, Goddamn it, I didn't put it there."

Chief Banks said, "Well, you stick around home, don't leave. I'll put a couple of men out after your wife. Willie must have known something, to be knocked off like this. Willie hasn't been working lately, and he has been coming up with quite a bit of money lately, too."

I said, "Okay, but don't you expect me to just sit here while those men have my wife."

He said, "Well, whatever you do, keep in touch. Let's get out of here, Frank."

They left, with the chief giving Frank orders on what to do.

I couldn't figure out why someone would want to ice Willie. He never bothered anybody. Sure, he had gotten laid off from work about six months ago, but he never bothered anybody for anything, because he didn't have anyone to look after but himself. He lived in a little house in the heart of the black neighborhood and everybody liked him, even the kids.

I went into the girls' room to check on how they were coming along. They had just about finished cleaning their room. They promised to have it done by the time their mother got home.

I said, "That's a good idea."

I left and went out and got the rest of the gifts off the back of the truck and brought them into the house. The rest of the afternoon was spent trying to get the house back in order. It was around seven twenty-five when we finished.

I said, "Okay, tomorrow we'll put up the Christmas tree.

That is, providing you two go in, get your shower, and hit the sack."

From that I didn't get any back talk. After they had gotten settled down for the night, I looked in the closet and got out my 30-30, along with my shotgun. I loaded them and put them in different rooms. Then I took a shower and lay down on the couch. I still hadn't heard from Tom. Just as I sat down the phone started ringing. I was hoping it was Ruby. I said, "Hello." It was Chief Banks.

He said, "Don't go to bed, Tommie, I want to talk to you."

I said, "Come on, I'm still up. Have you heard anything from my wife?"

He said, "Not a word, but the guys are still looking. See you in a few minutes."

It wasn't like Tom not to call, so I decided to call the joint. The line was busy. I waited for about five minutes and tried again. Somebody answered the phone. I said, "Is Tom there?" They said, "No" and hung up. About that time there was a knock on the door. I got my shotgun and slowly walked over to the door.

I said, "Who is it?"

Chief Banks said, "It's me, Tommie."

I opened the door still holding the shotgun in my hand.

He said, "You can put that away, you won't need it."

I said, "Hell, I put it under my pillow every night. Now what in the hell are you trying to pin on me, Chief? Murder?"

He said, "Just hold on, Tommie, there is more. Willie died about three hours before you got home. We checked your story out about the shopping, and it was okay. Willie wasn't killed here at your house—it was done someplace else. First, there wasn't enough blood on the kitchen floor and, second, he had red clay on his shoes and clothing. Now, if it's something you are not telling me, Tommie, you better start now. I had in mind to book you this afternoon but this came in from the lab and shined a different light on things."

I said, "Chief, I am just as far from this thing as I was just a day ago when it all got started. When you came in and marched me off the job I was lost then. I get the hell beaten out of me, my wife gets kidnapped, Willie gets knocked off, and would you believe I am still in the dark?"

He said, "Somebody is trying awfully hard to make you look like our man, but it's something I just can't quite pin down. We don't have a damn thing to go on and that makes me mad. Well, that's all for the night, come down to the station tomorrow and we will talk some more."

I said, "I'll be there, but if you get any word on Ruby, call me."

He said, "Will do."

The next morning the girls wanted to know why their mother hadn't come home.

I said, "Well, she might have stayed over to Clara's. She will come home later. Now you guys promised to help me put up the tree. Is it still a deal?"

They said, "Okay."

So that is how it went for the rest of the day, and still not a word from Ruby and the kidnappers. The girls wanted to talk about their mother not being home and not calling. I started to try to make another excuse, but it didn't work.

Coleidia said, "Daddy, we know it is something wrong. You were beaten up and tied up when we came home yesterday and the police keep coming here, and now mommy is gone."

I said, "Well, it may be. . ."

Loleadia cut me off. She said, "Daddy, why don't you want to tell us what's wrong?" Then she started to cry.

I said, "Okay, okay." I took her and the other one in my arms. I said, "You girls are right, something is wrong, but I don't know what. I don't even know where your mother is. As soon as somebody tells me what's going on, we'll all know. Right now, daddy is in the dark. I'm going to call grandma to come over to stay with you guys. Daddy's got something to do, so you guys go and get your showers and wait for grandma."

They said, "Okay," but I know they were not pleased.

I picked up the phone and dialed Mrs. Etta Morgan's number (that was Ruby's mother) and told her to come to the house right away. I told her I would explain it all when she got here. She was trying to ask me something, but I hung up the phone.

I stood there looking down at the phone wondering why Tom hadn't called me. He hadn't even stopped by, and that was strange for Tom. I picked up the phone and dialed his number. I slowly put the phone back on the receiver. Then I lifted it back up and dialed another friend of mine—Ronney Maker. His wife, Clara, answered the phone.

I said, "Clara, this is Tommie. Is Ronney there?"

She said, "Yes, but he is busy."

I said, "Well, tell him to get unbusy. I've got to talk to him."

She said, "Now, Tommie, we don't want to get in no trouble."

I said, "Look, what the hell gives? I call and ask to speak to Ronney and you start clamping up. What's wrong with you, girl? Let me talk to Ronney."

She was about to say something when Ronney said, "Give me the phone, woman."

She said, "Now Ronney. . ."

He said, "Shut up, woman, and go on. Tommie, this is me, man, what is happening, blood?"

I said, "I have got to talk to you, man."

He said, "Well, you know where I live—come on over. I'll be here."

I could hear Clara in the background trying to say something when he hung up the phone. As I was hanging up the phone, Mr. and Mrs. Morgan were at the door. I let them in.

I said, "I'm not stalling for time, I've got something to do. Mr. Morgan, I know you heard what happened on the job the other day and also what happened to Willie Wright. Well, right now Ruby has been kidnapped. The people who took her think I have the rest of that stuff they put in my car, and they said if I didn't come up with it I wouldn't see Ruby again."

Mrs. Morgan said, "Oh, my God—what are you going to do, Tommie?"

I said, "Right now I am going to try and find Ruby. That's all I can tell you now because that is all I know."

I kissed the girls and said, "If Tom calls, tell him I am over to Ronney's house. Be seeing you. Good-bye."

I got in the pickup and headed out. After about three blocks, I noticed the same car that pulled out just after I did was still following. I acted like I didn't notice. When I got to Ronney's house, they parked at the end of the block. When I knocked on the door, Ronney opened it.

He said, "Come on in, man. How come you haven't been in touch."

I said, "I don't know, but, man, everything's been going wrong. I got beaten up at home yesterday about four-thirty, and the guys that did it kidnapped Ruby. They said if I didn't come up with their stuff, I wouldn't see her alive again. I think it's the same two guys who followed me over here."

He said, "I don't care about them following you here, just so they don't try to come in." He said, "Now, what do you want me to do?"

I said, "Help me find Ruby."

He said, "You got it. When do we start? Maybe those two cats who followed you over here can give us a start."

Clara said, "Now, Ronney, don't you. . ."

He said, "Just shut up, woman, and get out of here." He said, "What you say, let's find out what those two birds know? Do you remember the way we used to outsmart those cats? What do you say let's turn the calendar back a few years."

I said, "You know me. I am all for it."

He said, "You always could play drunk better than I could—you take the back door."

He said, "Hey, wait a minute." He reached up on the shelf and got down his bottle, and said, "After you, man."

We both took a drink and were on our way. I had the bottle under my arm, when I rounded the corner. I began to stagger. Just before I got to the car where the two guys were sitting, I took another drink out of the bottle. I capped the bottle and staggered over by the side of the car. I lay across the hood. The guy on the right side said, "Okay, fellows, move along."

I said, "Just who in the hell is going to make me?"

I made my way around to the door where he was.

I said, "Are you going to make me, buddy?"

I took another drink from the bottle. Then I started banging on the hood. The guy on the right side got out and came over to where I was. I let him have one in the guts. Before he could get a word out I followed through with a knee to the chin. He dropped to the ground. Meanwhile Ronney had jerked the door open on the left side and had laid one into the other guy's jaw. When the guy fell, Ronney reached inside his coat and took out a .38 special. It didn't dawn on me that the one I had hit was carrying a piece, too. I took one out from this guy's coat, just like the one Ronney had. The one I hit was out cold. I looked over at Ronney and he was sitting on his guy's stomach. He had the gun he had taken from him pointed right at the guy's nose.

He said, "Okay, punk, now where is Tommie's wife?"

He said, "I don't know what the hell you are talking about, but you are in a lot of trouble now, boy."

I walked over and said, "You are the one in trouble if you don't tell me where my wife is."

I went over and got the other guy and twisted his arm up behind his back.

I said, "Maybe you can tell me where my wife is. If you don't, buster, you won't be using this arm for a long time."

He said, "We're F.B.I. agents."

I said, "Yes, and I'm Santa Claus. I just don't have my reindeer with me tonight."

About that time I heard sirens. A few people had begun to gather. Chief Banks, I knew, was on his way, and I was giving these two birds to him. The guy on the ground told Ronney to look inside his coat pocket and get his I.D.

Ronney said, "And don't you move."

He reached inside the guy's pocket and took out his folder. He said, "Well, I'll be damned, the guy is right. He is a Fed."

I loosened the hold I had on the other guy's arm.

I said, "You fellows followed me over here tonight, and I had been beat up by two guys, so I thought you were the ones."

About that time Chief Banks was there.

He said, "What in the hell is going on here?"

I said, "We made a mistake, chief."

The guy on the ground said, "You're damn right you did. Chief, I want these two men locked up for assault on a federal officer."

I handed the guy his gun.

I said, "These two guys followed me from my house and I thought they were the ones who beat me up and kidnapped my wife, so Ronney and I thought we would make them tell where she was."

Chief Banks said, "Well, you two were wrong. Now I got

some bad news for you. One of the sheriff's deputies that rides back out on the old Back Irland roads found your wife and the two guys that took her. All three of them were dead. They shot the two guys while they sat in the car, and went around and put five holes in the trunk where Ruby was tied up. It was done with a high-powered rifle. Your wife never knew what hit her. I'm sorry, Tommie. I am going to have to ask you to come down and identify the body."

The two Feds said, "Well, we are going to forget about that charge this time, just don't let it happen again. We are sorry about your wife." Then they left.

I lay my head across the hood of Chief Banks's car and began to cry.

Ronney said, "Chief, I'll see that he comes down later, okay?"

He said, "Okay, Ronney."

He looked at Frank and said, "Let's get the hell out of here."

Ronney said, "Come on over to the house and let's have some coffee."

When we reached the door, Clara said, "See what I told you, you are goin'. . ."

Ronney cut in and said, "Clara, Ruby is dead."

She said, "Oh, my God, no. Oh, Tommie, I am sorry."

Ronney said, "Now, Clara, if you don't have something nice to say for a change, shut your goddamn mouth; and that I won't repeat, okay?"

She then began to cry.

I said, "It's okay, Clara, you were only thinking about your family. I understand."

Ronney said, "I'll drive you down to the station."

We left in Ronney's car. On the way down I was trying to think of what I was going to tell the kids and Mrs. Morgan and her husband. It all got to me. I began to cry. Ronney didn't say a word. We reached the station and Frank led me back to the morgue. He reached in and pulled out a slab and unwrapped the head.

I said, "It's Ruby. That's my wife."

Ronney said, "Can we have a look at the other two?"

Frank showed us the bodies. I couldn't remember seeing them around town. The ones that beat me up had masks on.

Frank said, "These two guys never killed your wife, they both were shot from some distance away. They were hit with a bullet from the same high-powered rifle, but the shots that were fired into the trunk were shot from close range, also from the same gun. Now don't let the chief know I told you all this, but it looks as if your wife knew who knocked off Willie and who was at your house."

About that time we looked up and saw Chief Banks heading our way.

Frank said, "Now, Tommie, you just let me know who to release the body to, okay?"

I said, "Okay."

Then Ronney and I left for my house.

When we got there Mr. and Mrs. Morgan were still up. The girls had gone to bed. Mrs. Morgan knew something was wrong when we went in.

She said, "Tommie, what is it?"

I said, "Mrs. Morgan," but she cut me off, saying, "It's Ruby, isn't it?"

I said, "Yes, ma'am, she is dead."

She said, "Oh, my God, I knew it, I just knew it. I felt it all afternoon."

After a while, I finally told them both what had happened, and how it happened.

Ronney said, "Tommie, I am going to leave you folks. I better get home and see how Clara and the kids are. I'll be around the house all day, so call me if you need anything."

I said, "Okay, Ronney, see you later."

I told Mr. Morgan that I would break the news to the girls in the morning.

The next morning I broke the news to the girls, and as I knew, they took it hard.

Clara must have spread the news all over town, because by ten o'clock the house was full.

I called Ronney and told him to pick me up.

He said, "Be right there," and hung up.

Then I dialed Tom's number. After about three rings, Betty answered the phone.

I said, "Betty, this is Tommie, is Tom home?"

She hesitated for a moment, then she said, "No, he's not, Tommie. Didn't Tom tell you he was going out of town?' He said he would be gone for two weeks."

I said, "No, he didn't. Did he leave any money with you for me?"

She said, "No, he didn't. He and Willie Wright left here. I heard what happened to Willie, now I haven't heard from Tom."

I said, "Willie and Tom were together?"

She said, "Yes, and they were on the way to your house."

I said, "Thanks, Betty. If I hear anything, I'll let you know. Meanwhile, did Tom say where he was going?"

She said, "Yes, he was going down to Memphis, Tennessee. Said something about buying some new equipment for the place. Said he had a good deal on it."

Ronney was outside blowing his horn. I told Mr. and Mrs. Morgan I would be right back, and if anybody called, to tell them I'd call them back. Then I left.

It was only three days before Christmas. The streets were full of shoppers in that little town. Ronney and I headed over to Mayberry Funeral Home. We went in and I arranged the funeral for Christmas Eve; then we headed over to the police station to see Chief Banks.

When we got there, Chief Banks said, "I was hoping you'd stop by."

I said, "What for—more bad news?"

He said, "No, for a change, good news. The Narcs dropped the charges against you. I went over and talked to Leavydon and he agreed to give you your job back. He said take off all the time you need. He also gave me these to give you."

He handed me two checks. One was my payroll check and the other one was for the little bonus we got every year.

I said, "Thanks, Chief. Now what about Willie, my wife, and the other two fellows?"

He said, "We are still working on that, and so far we have come up with zero."

I said, "Thanks, anyway, chief. Christmas sure brought me one helluva Christmas gift."

Then Ronney and I left. We got in the car and headed over to Ronney's house.

I said, "Ronney, it's something wrong somewhere."

While we talked, we broke open the half pint Ronney kept in the glove box.

I said, "First, Willie was killed and brought to my house. That means Willie knew who the middleman was who was supposed to have picked up the stuff. Ruby had to know who it was, too, so whoever it was took everybody out of the picture that knew."

Suddenly Ronney pulled over to the curb.

He said, "Didn't I hear you say that Willie and Tom left his house together that day he was killed?"

I said, "That's what Betty said."

He said, "Tommie, I been doing some thinking ever since you told me that. How do Tommie Foley and Tom Moley sound?"

I said, "Man, you got to be crazy—not Tom. It couldn't be."

He said, "Remember when we were little we used to go out back of Tom's daddy's house and play in that old red dirt? Well, Willie had red dirt on his clothes, and the chief said he was killed someplace other than your house. He and Tom were together after you went out and got his pickup, and nobody has seen Tom since Willie was killed. The stuff was supposed to go to Memphis, and where is Tom?"

I sat there stunned as hell at what Ronney was saying; it all made sense. Ronney pulled off and we headed on over to his house. Neither one of us said a word.

We got to his house, Ronnie said, "Come on in, Tommie, and get yourself together."

I said, "That son of a bitch—I even gave him my twenty-five hundred bucks to keep. I told him to put it in his safe deposit box; now the bastard has left town, at least that's what his wife said." I said, "Ronney, I'll be in touch. I got some checking to do—see you later."

When I got home everybody had gone. The girls came to me and started crying all over again. I told them the funeral was Christmas Eve. Mrs. Morgan said she had contacted all the folks. I didn't have anybody but a brother, and I hadn't seen him since he was twelve years old and I didn't know how to get in touch with him.

I picked up the phone and dialed Tom's number. Betty answered.

I said, "Betty, this is Tommie again." I asked her did she hear from Tom.

She said, "No, not yet."

I told her what time the funeral was; she said she would be there and hung up.

Somehow the Christmas spirit was all over for me. I knew it wouldn't be a good Christmas at home for the girls, so I told them we would spend the Christmas with Ronney and his family. They said that would be fine.

It was getting late in the evening. I walked out on the back porch. Far across the fields you could see Christmas lights. I stood there taking in the view. Suddenly I could taste the salty tears in the corner of my mouth. Then the wind began to chill the tears on my cheeks. I took my handkerchief and wiped my eyes and went back inside.

Mr. and Mrs. Morgan's family had just begun to come in. Everybody was broken up. That's the way it went until I fell asleep on the couch.

I got up the next morning and dressed and had a cup of coffee before anybody else got up. While I was sitting there drinking my coffee I was thinking about what Ronney had said about Tom. Somehow I knew it wasn't like Tom to spend the Christmas away from his family, but I decided to wait until after the funeral to try getting in touch with him. The more I thought about it the more it made sense. Tom was always a fast thinker when it came to money. With my name being Tommie Foley and his being Tom Moley, it was very easy that Tom could have taken the stuff and told them that I had it. Then by planting some in my car and lunch box and tipping off the police, could easily point the pickup men on to me. Using Willie to do the dirty work, he couldn't take the chance that Willie would stick it out, knowing that he and I were very close, too. Ruby must have come home at the wrong time and caught what had gone down at my house, so they killed her, too, along with the two guys that were here to pick the stuff up, and now he was home free with the stuff, and if there was any comeback on it from Memphis, they would come looking for Tommie Foley, so I was right back where I started out—in the middle. The more I thought about it the madder I got. Had Tom really gone to Memphis, or was he still home and having Betty say he was out of town? I didn't know, but after the funeral, I was sure as hell going to find out, and Tom was also going to give me my twenty-five hundred bucks.

The funeral was held the next day, Christmas Eve. Seems like everybody in town came. Funny how people act in a small town. It seemed like no one had any Christmas spirit, even after the funeral. The ones who came to the house didn't mention Christmas, but just about all the ones that came brought a gift for the girls.

We decided to spend the Christmas with Ronney and his family, but later that evening Ronney and Clara brought their two kids, Dickey and Jeffery, over to spend the holiday with us. Ronney and I went over to Mrs. Morgan's and got their gifts and brought them over, too. We put the kids to bed early. Ronney and I started popping the tops on a few bottles of booze.

After the kids were asleep, we started opening the gifts and putting toys together. You would have thought the living room was a department store.

The next morning came fast. The kids were into the toys like crazy and having a good time. I had already taken my shotgun, along with a dozen double-O bucks, and put them out on the back porch. I didn't tell anyone that I was going to find Tom that day. Around nine o'clock Frank brought my car back. I asked him to have a drink. He said, "No, the chief is right behind me, and I am on duty today." Just about that time the chief drove up.

He said, "Merry Christmas, Tommie."

I said, "Same to you."

He said, "We haven't come up with a thing; when we do you will be the first to know."

I said, "Thanks, chief. Won't you come in?"

He said, "No, got work to do, but see you later."

I went back inside. Everyone seemed to be having a nice time. Coleidia and Loleadia were having a good time. For a moment I felt good. Mrs. Morgan had taken all of Ruby's gifts and put them in the other room.

I couldn't fool Ronney. He knew something was on my mind. He walked over to me and said, "Okay, let's have it."

I said, "There's nothing to tell."

He said, "Tommie, this is Ronney, remember? You know you never could lie to me and hold a straight face behind it. Now come on—let's have it. Now you know I am going to hound you until you give, so you might as well save us some time."

I took a deep breath. I said, "Ronney, somehow I don't believe Tom is out of town and the only way I am going to know is go out there and see for myself."

He said, "Don't you think you should tell Chief Banks about what you got in mind?"

I said, "No, Ronney, I got to find this out for myself. I don't want the police looking for Tom if my guess is wrong."

He said, "What if your guess is right?"

I said, "Well, we just have to wait and see."

Ronney took a long breath and said, "You know, if Tom is in on this thing he is not going to let you go back to the police. I think I better come along, too."

I said, "No, I don't want you mixed up in this. You stay close to the phone in case I need you."

He said, "Why don't you wait until tomorrow?"

I said, "I got to know today. If it's any day he is home, it's today."

He said, "Okay, Tommie, but be careful. Four people are dead already."

I said, "Do me a favor, and don't tell anybody where I am going."

He said, "You got it."

I got my coat and hat and left by the back door, picking up my shotgun and shells from off the porch. I went around the house and got in the car. I took a look around. It was a perfect day for a Christmas. A few flakes of snow had fallen that night, and from the looks of the clouds, more were coming. I took a deep breath and pulled off.

Just before I got to the road leading to Tom's house, I turned off on the old side road leading up the back way. The ditch would conceal the car from being seen from the house. I parked the car just before I reached the high side of the ditch. I reached in the glove box and got out my binoculars. Tom's house was only about six hundred yards from where I was. I took a look around the house. Tom's car was nowhere in sight. His wife's car was parked in the driveway. I started to take the glasses down when I noticed smoke coming from Betty's car's tailpipe. It seemed that she was getting ready to leave. I said to myself, now that would make things easy. I took another look—she was coming toward the car with some Christmas gifts in her arms. Suddenly I had to take a double look—it was Tom. He was carrying her handbag in one hand and his rifle in the other one. I almost said aloud—he's expecting me. He couldn't know I was coming. Nobody knew I was coming but Ronney. Betty had been lying all the time when she said he was in Memphis, Tennessee. He had been here all the time, and nobody knew I was on my way out here but Ronney.

I said, "That dirty son of a bitch, he tipped Tom off." All that about how the thing might have been came from him. He could be in on the Goddamn thing, too.

Betty got in her car and left. Just as she got down the road a ways, there was a police car pulled up in the drive. I got the glasses and took a better look. It was Frank. Tom came out on the porch. They stood there for a few minutes—then Tom went back to the house. Frank got in the patrol car and pulled it up inside the garage and closed the door. He had his riot gun in his hand. He went into the house with Tom.

I said, "Well, I'll be a dirty bastard. Frank was in on it, too, and Ronney wanted me to go to Chief Banks. That son of a bitch might be in on it, too." I wasn't going to try to take them by myself, and again I didn't know anybody to turn to.

I went back to the car, got in and started the engine. Just as I began to back out, I noticed Ronney's car pulling up behind me. I grabbed my shotgun and rolled out the right door. When he stopped I had the shotgun aimed right at his head.

I said, "Keep your Goddamn hands on the steering wheel or I'll blow that front glass right through your head."

I waited until he killed the motor, then I walked between the front of his car and the back of mine. I was still holding the shotgun straight at his head.

I said, "I hope you try something so I can blow your ass to hell. You tipped Tom off, didn't you?"

He said, "You want the truth? Nope, I didn't tip Tom off."

I said, "Don't lie, Ronney, you were the only one who knew that I was coming out here."

He said, "Will you lower that damn thing—it's making me nervous."

I said, "I just hope you try something."

He said, "Tommie, I didn't tip Tom off. Now if you lower that Goddamn thing I got something to tell you."

I said, "Go ahead, I can listen just as good with you looking down the barrel."

Ronney took a long breath and let it out.

He said, "Tommie, your two girls are dead. So is your father-in-law."

I said, "What did you say?"

He said, "Your two girls are dead. Coleidia and Loleadia." By then he was crying.

I slowly lowered the shotgun, then it fell to the ground.

I said, "My little girls—no, it can't be. How? Why? You're lying to me, Ronney. Tell me you're lying."

He said, "Tommie, I wish I was, my God, I wish I was."

I said, "What happened?"

He said, "Tommie, it happened so fast nobody could believe it. All I remember was that Mr. Morgan said he was going to check on the house. He went out the door, started the motor in his car and came back in the house. He told the twins he could be right back. One of them said, 'Can we go with you, granddaddy?' I don't know which one it was. I never could tell them apart. He told her, 'Yes, but go get your coats and don't forget your gloves.' He said to me, 'Ronney, I might as well drive Tom's truck, it's behind my car.' He told the girls that they were going to go in the pickup. So they left out the door. Everybody was talking and having fun, and all of a sudden *bang*. Everybody got quiet. I rushed to the door and opened it, and there it was—the truck was blown to bits, and covered with flames. I tried to get to the truck, but the flames drove me back. I yelled for someone to call the fire department. Lawrence grabbed the water hose. We tried to get enough water on the fire to pull them out, but we couldn't. When Chief Banks got there he opened the trunk and took out some fire extinguishers. He said Jake had run for the fire extinguishers and came as quick as he could. But, Tommie, when we did get it down enough to look inside, man, we didn't know who was who. They never knew what hit them. It was bad to look at."

About that time I was shaking all over. Ronney walked over and picked the shotgun up off the ground. I didn't know what to say. I couldn't walk. I just kept saying over and over, "No, not my little girls, no, no."

Finally Ronney said, "You're in no shape to drive, Tommie. I'll park my car over there behind those willow trees and I'll drive you back to town. I've taken Mrs. Morgan over to my house. The doctor is with her."

Ronney took the shotgun and laid it across the trunk of my car where I was.

He said, "Tommie, I didn't tip Tom off. If I was going to, I would have told him which way you were coming in."

I said, "I know how Tom knew I was coming. Frank told him. Frank was in on the whole thing. He's got his car parked inside Tom's garage now, and they both are waiting inside for me. The boom was meant for me. They missed. That's why Frank came out to warn Tom. Somehow I wish it had been me."

I was beginning to get mad. Ronney could see it.

He said, "Come on, Tommie, we'll do like we used to do in the old days. When somebody had the best hand, we went back and regrouped. That's what we got to do now. You only have this shotgun, and I don't have anything, and, man, those cats are dealing with high-power stuff, and let's face it. Tom is out to get you out of the way. Because if Frank is in with him, he knows you are going to get even with him, so let's get the hell out of here and do some thinking."

I said, "All right, we'll go, but you can believe on my grave, I am coming back."

Ronney took his car and parked it just off the turn road a little piece, then we got in my car and left.

I said, "Don't stop at my house, I don't want to see where Coleidia and Loleadia spent their last Christmas."

We headed straight to Ronney's house. The news had gotten over town about what had happened, because when we got there people were coming from all over town. We sat in the car for a little while. Neither one of us said a word. I was just sitting there thinking about what to do.

Finally I said to Ronney, "Let's go inside."

We met Dr. Jameson at the door.

He said, "I am sorry, son, your mother-in-law is going to be all right, but she will have to be kept quiet, and for God's sake don't let her attend the funeral. She almost didn't make it through this. God only knows what will happen if she goes to the funeral."

I said, "Thanks, Dr. Jameson, but there won't be any funeral."

Everybody looked at me.

I said, "That's right, there won't be any funeral. I don't think I could stand another one myself. I am going to call George Lome and have him meet me at the cemetery. Ronney and I are going to take Ruby her two little girls. I think it will make her happy that she didn't spend the Christmas alone. She and the girls can spend it together. She will understand. Mrs. Morgan can't stand another funeral, either, so I am going to take Mr. Morgan along so he can look after them."

Ronney said, "You're sure that's what you want to do, Tommie?"

I said, "I'm sure. I don't want anybody to come along but Ronney." Then I asked, "Ronney, would you help me take care of this?"

Ronney was wiping tears from his eyes, but he said, "Come on, man, and don't ask crazy questions."

After we were outside, I said, "I didn't think you would after the way I treated you out there on the turn road. I owe you one for that."

Ronney said, "I must admit, it's hell when you're looking down a gun barrel."

I said, "Hold it a minute. I got to get in touch with George."

I went back in the house and called George. I told him what I wanted.

He said, "Man, on Christmas Day? The funeral won't be until next week. What's the rush?"

I said, "George, there won't be any funeral. I am going to take the kids out to Ruby so they can spend the rest of this

Christmas together. Now, if you don't want to do it I'll get somebody else, and if I can't—I'll dig the graves myself."

He said, "No. No, don't worry. I'll take care of it. Give me about two hours." Then he hung up.

Then I called Mr. Herman Beck. I told him what I wanted to do.

He said, "Okay, Tommie, I understand. I'll go and get things ready. I'm not going to leave the caskets open. I know you don't want to see what's left."

I said, "Thanks, Mr. Beck."

He said, "Give me about a half-hour. Well, you better make it an hour."

I said, "See you in about an hour-and-a-half."

Ronney and I left. We got in the car and for a long time neither one of us said a word. Finally Ronney broke the silence.

He said, "What's next after you bury your folks?"

I said, "Have a talk with Tom and Frank."

He said, "Don't you think we should get hold of Chief Banks?"

I said, "I'm not sure he's not in on the whole thing, too."

He said, "It sounds like you are going to do more than talk to them."

I said, "If it takes more than talk to get to the bottom of things, then that's what it will be."

Ronney said, "Tommie, if it's killing, I want no part of it."

I said, "Nobody is asking you."

He said, "What if Chief Banks is in on the deal?"

I said, "I'll have to talk with him, too."

Ronney shook his head and said, "Man, you're crazy."

I said, "I have already lost everything I ever lived for. I don't have a Goddamn thing else to lose."

He said, "I guess it's no use telling you not to, is it?"

I said, "Not one bit."

He said, "I thought so."

I said, "While we're out, let's stop by Mr. Morgan's house. I want to check on things."

When we reached the house, Ronney said, "You want me to go in with you?"

I said, "No, I just want to check the house out."

I took the key and went in. I knew where Mr. Morgan kept

his guns. I took out the .357 magnum. It was fully loaded. I reached in the drawer and took out a handful of the .357 millimeter shells and stuck them in my pocket. I stuck the pistol in my belt and turned the living room light on. I took the mail out of the box and put it on the coffee table. I turned the porch light on and left.

We headed over to the funeral home. Mr. Beck was waiting. He said he had everything in order.

I said, "I will bring you the insurance papers over tomorrow."

He said, "Don't worry yourself about that, son. I am in no hurry. I am just glad I can help you take care of things today."

I said, "Thanks for everything."

We loaded the caskets in the back of the truck. I got into the truck with Mr. Beck. Ronney followed in his car.

George was just finishing digging the graves when we got there.

I said, "How much do I owe you, George?"

He said, "Nothing, Tommie. Barbara would have never let me out of the house if she knew I charged you."

Folding up two twenties, I said, "Then don't tell her a thing." I shoved the money in his coat pocket and said, "Thanks for everything, pal."

George helped us take the caskets off the truck. The two pink ones were my twins. Mr. Beck had put Mr. Morgan in a dark blue one. He said, "Old Morgan was always crazy about blue."

We lowered the two pinks, one on each side of Ruby's grave, and put Mr. Morgan up at the head of them.

I said, "Don't worry. Ruby will know which one is which."

After they were all lowered in the ground, I stood at the front of Ruby's grave.

I said, "Darling, I am bringing the girls over to spend the rest of this Christmas with you. I knew you would be lonely spending the Christmas out here alone. I even brought your father along to look after you girls. I didn't have time to stop and get you a gift. The girls can tell you about the ones we left at the house. I know your Christmas is going to be a much happier one with the girls here with you. Merry Christmas, darling, and take care of the kids."

I walked over to Mr. Morgan's grave.

I said, "Mr. Morgan, I know you understand why I am doing things this way. Now don't start frowning because I took your gun. You know what I got to do. I'll be leaving town when it's all over, but I'll be back to look in on you, Ruby and the kids."

I walked back over to the truck and let it all out. Nobody spoke a word. When I looked around, Mr. Beck was saying a few words over the graves. When he finished, he just got in his truck and left. He was crying, too. In fact, everybody was crying. George got on his digger and covered up the graves. Just before we left, Ronney walked over to Ruby's grave and said, "Don't worry, Ruby, I'll look after him."

We got in the car and left. Ronney reached in the back seat and got his jug.

He said, "Here, you need one."

I said, "In fact we both need one."

He said, "You all right?"

I said, "I'm fine. Take me by the house, I'll explain to everybody why I did what I did."

He said, "You won't have to—they all understand."

The sun had just ducked out of sight. People had begun to turn on the Christmas lights. Ronney said, "Tommie, let's go out and get drunk tonight? What do you say?"

I said, "Not tonight, Ronney, I got something to do."

He said, "Well, here's to you, and good luck." He took a long pull on the bottle.

By then we had made it to the house. We got out and went inside. There were only a few people there.

Clara said, "Let me fix you something to eat, Tommie, and I won't take no for an answer. So you just sit down."

I said, "It's a deal, but I want to talk to Mrs. Morgan."

Ronney was feeling pretty good. He said, "Hey, baby, what about yours truly?"

She said, "You will get to eat because Tommie is."

He said, "Well, well, what a difference a day makes." He shook the bottle at her and said, "See, old woman, I still got a friend."

Everybody laughed.

Henry flipped the hi-fi on. I went into the room where Mrs.

Morgan was. She said, "Come on in, Tommie. I am not asleep. Come on over and sit by the bed." She said, "Now before you start explaining why you did what you did today, just let me say I understand. Louis wouldn't have wanted it any other way. I am sure it made him happy."

I said, "Thanks, Mrs. Morgan, that's a big load off my chest. It was all I could think of."

She said, "No, it wasn't. You were thinking about me, too, Tommie, and I am glad. But, Tommie, I've been sleeping and not sleeping and I been hearing things said out front I didn't like to hear."

She said, "Tommie, I was just as much responsible for raising you and Tom as your uncles and aunts were. In fact, we all felt like we should contribute to making you two a good home after both your mothers and fathers were killed in that accident coming from a church convention in Memphis, and I don't believe any of this talk I've been hearing out front. Have you talked to Tom yet?"

I said, "No, mama, I haven't, but I plan to go out and see him tonight."

She said, "Good, maybe you two can clear up all these rumors. What are you planning on doing now, Tommie?"

I said, "After this is all over, I guess I will sell the house. I only lack about two years from having it paid for. I'll give away the things in it. Maybe somebody around Hayti can use them. Then I probably will head north—Chicago, New York, somewhere I can make a new start. I just know I have to get away from here."

She said, "I understand, and I won't try to make you stay, but don't you forget to write."

I said, "Hold on, I haven't gone yet."

She said, "Well, I knew you were going to do something like that, but you go out there and talk to Tom and straighten things out with him."

I said, "That's what I am going to do tonight. Now you get some rest, and quit worrying and don't worry about going home, you're just as much at home here at Clara's and Ronney's as you were at your own house." I bent down and kissed her on the forehead and said goodnight. She didn't say anything, but somehow her eyes told me she didn't believe I was going just to talk with Tom, so I just left the room without another word.

Clara caught me as I came out of the room.

She said, "You get in that kitchen and eat. Ronney has already got a head start."

She marched me in the kitchen and set me down. Once I started eating, I was kind of glad she did. I didn't know how hungry I was.

It was around seven forty-five when I finished. I came out and made me a small drink and settled down in the lounge chair and kicked off my shoes. I didn't only relax, I went to sleep. It was around ten o'clock when I woke up. Everybody was still having a good time. Ronney was in the corner asleep.

I got my coat and told everybody I was leaving. I told Clara not to wake Ronney up. I said Merry Christmas and left.

I got to the car and opened the trunk. I had stashed me a fifth of Old Grand Dad inside. I took it out and popped the top, taking a long pull. I cleared my throat and took a short pull. I sat the bottle in the front seat beside me. I started the engine and let it run for about five minutes. Just before I pulled off, I took another long drink from the bottle.

I took my time driving out to Tom's house. Just before I reached the house, I turned the lights out, then drove past the house. I noticed that there was only one light on, and that was the Christmas tree. I went down to an old turn road and turned around. I didn't see Tom's or Betty's car. I sat there thinking how I was going to get in the house without being seen. I walked down to the garage and had a look inside. There was Betty's car parked in the garage. I went back to the car. Going in Tom's driveway was a little downhill. I rolled the car down to the top of the hill and stopped. I got out and took my bumper jack stand and put it under the front wheel to keep the car from rolling, then I tied the clothesline cord to it. I got the .357 magnum from under the seat and stuck it in my belt. I walked around to the back door holding the string in my hand. I had angled the car to roll right against the bedroom side of the house. I took my knife and cut the screen just over the lock of the screen door. Then I reached inside and opened the door. I took the catch and propped it open. I took the .357 magnum from my belt. I knew I was only going to get one chance to break the door in, so I said to myself, "Tommie, you got to make do with all two hundred and twenty pounds."

I picked up the string and backed up about six feet. I tightened the string up, then shifted the .357 magnum over to my right hand, then gave the string a yank, letting the car roll; about time it got to the house it had a good start. When the car rammed the side of the house, I hit the back door with all I had. When I fell inside, I scrambled to my feet and headed toward the bedroom. Just as I got almost to the door, it popped open and Tom was coming out in a rush with his Winchester in his hand, and Betty was right behind him. He had his back to me—I could see him plain with the bedroom light from inside. I jammed the .357 magnum in his neck. I said, "One move, dead man. Now drop it."

He froze.

I said, "You either drop it in two seconds or I'll blow the back of your head off. One." Before I could say two, the rifle hit the floor. I said, "I just hope you rouse me some way so I can fuck you off."

Betty was trying to get her housecoat on. She said, "Tommie, what in the world came over you?"

I said, "Just shut up and come on out of the room. For Tom's sake I hope you don't try anything funny. I only need one excuse to pull this trigger, and Tom, for your information, this is Mr. Morgan's old .357 magnum. Remember how he used to show us how it had a hair trigger? Well, my finger is laying on it."

He began to shake, then I pulled the hammer back. Tom's knees almost buckled.

I said, "Both of you move ahead of me, and when you get in the living room, you belly down on the floor—now move."

Tom said, "Tommie, I can explain all of this."

I said, "Don't worry, you're going to."

I gave them a little shove. When they got in the living room they both got down on the floor.

I said, "Okay, you dirty son of a bitch, start talking."

Betty said, "He made me tell you he was out of town."

I said, "I don't want to hear a damn thing from you, Betty. Tom is the one I want to start talking, and you can start, buddy, by telling me where my twenty-five hundred bucks is."

He said, "It's in the briefcase behind the couch." I walked over and got the briefcase and snapped the lock open. For a minute I had to clear my eyes—the case was full of money—nothing but fives, tens and twenties.

Tom said, "Tommie, you can have half of what's there, two hundred twenty-five thousand bucks. All cash, no strings attached."

I said, "So you were in on the dope. No thanks, all I want is what belongs to me."

I counted out my money and closed the case up. I threw it down on the floor in front of him.

I said, "Okay, now start talking."

Tom said, "It was Frank's idea. He's been the relay man here in Hayti for sometime. All the stuff that came through going to Memphis was handled by Frank. He told me how we could take the whole haul. He said he would contact the man in Memphis and tell them that I had the stuff and that the heat was closing in on him. He said he would fill me in on the rest the next day, but he gave them your name instead. He planted the stuff in your car and Willie planted the stuff in your lunch bucket. He tipped off Chief Banks that you had the stuff, so Chief Banks called the Feds in. They had been working on the case for a while trying to find the relay man, so when they found it on you, that was enough to take the heat off Frank, but I didn't know that Frank had given your name until I heard about them busting you."

I asked, "Who iced Willie?"

For a moment he didn't say anything.

I asked again, "Who iced Willie?"

He said, "I did, I had to. Willie thought the stuff was all mine. He wouldn't settle for the seven thousand for planting the stuff in your lunch bucket, and said if he couldn't have twenty-five thousand more he would blow the whistle on us. So Frank said we had to get rid of him. I picked Willie up that morning after I let you have my truck and brought him out here. I tried to get him to see that there wasn't any more money and if he would leave town I would give him another two thousand from my share. He said he had found out how much the stuff was worth, and he wanted twenty-five thousand more or he would tell you how the stuff got in your car and lunch bucket. I told him I had some more money stashed down behind the house. He could have that until the big deal came through. We went down to the old red bed creek. Once we got there I shot him, got him in the car and carried him down to your place. When we got there the pickup men were there from Memphis to get the stuff. They were in the house roughing Ruby around trying to find out where you had put the stuff. Then Frank came up. I told him about Willie. We decided to put him in your house. Frank got your gun and wrapped it in a blanket and fired it one time out the back door, then he put it on the floor beside the icebox."

I said, "These same two guys were at my house when I got there—now who took Ruby?"

He said, "I brought Ruby back home with me. She knew the whole thing, so I kept her tied up in the guest room. Later Frank came out, along with the other two fellows. He said the other two guys were heading back to Memphis and he just wanted to take Ruby back home and that he would explain to her what would happen to her and you and the kids if she opened her mouth. They left here with her and that's the truth. She was put in the trunk of the car. Frank said Ruby swore she was going to have us arrested. He said he told the guys where to go and left following them. They went out to Black Irland. They drove down by the old bob pit and he pulled up on the hillside. He said he took his .3006 and shot both of them without warning. He then let five rounds go in the trunk where Ruby was tied up. He got his gloves, took out the keys and opened the trunk to see that Ruby was dead. He closed the trunk, put the keys back and headed back to town. He said nobody would start trying to match tireprints with a police car."

I said, "Who put the bomb in the truck?"

He said "That was Frank, too. I went along. We knew you would be using the pickup. We didn't count on Mr. Morgan getting in the truck. That was a slip-up. Tommie, we had gotten so far involved that the only thing we thought to do was get the people out of the way who could bring the rap down on us."

I said, "My daughters wouldn't have done you any harm."

He said, "That was a mistake, we weren't trying to hurt the

kids." He said, "The stuff was picked up yesterday, and that's the money from it. Now, Tommie, you can have my share; Betty and I wouldn't do you no harm. We'll just sell the house and leave town. Putting us in jail won't bring back your family. Man, you got enough to last you a lifetime."

I said, "Just like that, you want me to let you go? You murdered Willie; had my wife tied up and had her suffer before you killed her; you put a bomb in your truck and killed my two daughters and father-in-law—seven people lose their lives just because of your greediness for money—and you want me to say, that's okay, and let you go free? Not on your life. You son of a bitch, you're going to pay."

Suddenly I heard a car door slam, then someone knocked on the door. It was Frank.

He said, "Tom, are you okay?"

Tom said, "Tommie is here. He got me and Betty. I didn't tell him anything, Frank."

He said, "Just shut up, Tom. Tommie, come on out, maybe you and I can make a deal."

I said, "Just like you made a deal with my wife; just like you made a deal with my two girls and my father-in-law? No deals, Frank, I'm calling Chief Banks."

I started dialing the phone. About halfway through the number the phone went dead. I knew Frank had cut the line. I crawled over to the window just in time to see Frank getting in the trunk of his car.

Tom said, "Tommie, he will never let Betty and me out of here alive."

I said, "Frank doesn't intend on letting any of us out of here alive."

Tom said, "Maybe if I go out and talk to him and tell him he can have the money he'll let us go."

I said, "That's your friend. Go ahead, but Betty stays here."

Suddenly I smelled gas. I knew what was going on. Frank was either going to burn the house down on us or shoot us coming out.

Tom jumped up and ran to the door. He said, "Frank, I'm coming out. Tommie is holding Betty; we can make a deal."

I said, "Don't go out there, Tom."

About that time he jerked the door open. He said, "Frank,

it's me, Tom, look, let's . . ." He never got to finish. Frank let loose with a blast from his riot gun, then another one. Tom fell back in the door. He was almost cut in half. Betty began to scream. I looked out the window and tried to nail Frank before he ducked behind the car. Two shots—and I missed with both. I looked around and the flames were all over the back door. The smoke started coming in. I lost sight of Betty. I reached down, got the money and threw it out the side window. I could hear Betty near the front door coughing. I made it to her and pulled her back, but she couldn't take the smoke any longer. She pulled loose and went out the door. I heard two shots. Sounded like a Winchester—then I heard the sweetest voice this side of heaven. It was Ronney. I was trying to make my way to the front door. The flames were getting to me. I started crawling on the floor. Ronney was still yelling, "Tommie, Tommie, are you all right?"

I couldn't answer. Suddenly the lights went out. The next thing I knew I was breathing through a mask. I set up and Chief Banks said, "Aw, he'll be okay."

I said, "Chief, have you seen Frank?"

He said, "Don't worry about him, Ronney made sure he didn't get away. He got two bullet wounds, but he'll be all right."

I said, "How did you know I was out here?"

He said, "Mrs. Morgan called me and told me what she had been hearing, so I thought I better check it out."

I said, "Well, if you look on the other side of the house you'll find a briefcase full of money. Too bad about Tom, he tried to make a deal with Frank but got cut down, and by his so-called friend."

He said, "Ronney got the money, he was on that side of the house when you threw it out the window."

I said, "Well, you'll also find the rest of the stuff in Betty's car in the garage."

He told one of his men to get it out.

He said, "I'm sorry we couldn't have gotten this mess cleared up earlier. Too many good people are dead behind this. What a helluva Christmas Santa brought this time." He looked at Ronney and said, "I'm going to hold you responsible for getting Tommie down to the station tomorrow—maybe we can clear the air with all this mess." Then he left.

Ronney and I got in the car and headed for home. As usual, Ronney kept a nip on the back seat or somewhere. We popped the top and had a drink, and that's the way we made it home—passing the bottle.

Two days later Betty and Frank were bound over for trial. I knew I had to stay for that. She didn't even get to go to Tom's funeral, which was the day after New Year's. I didn't go myself.

Things were kind of lonely for the next two months waiting for the trial. In the meantime I sold my home and gave away the furniture. I took my old car and traded it in on a new one. Mrs. Morgan had gone to Chicago to live with one of her daughters for a while. She returned just two days before the trial. The trial lasted about four days. Betty was found guilty and given a ten-to-twelve-year sentence. Frank was also found guilty on six counts of murder in the first degree, along with two counts of distributing dangerous drugs. He drew six natural life sentences for murder in the first degree and two twenty-five-to-thirty-years for selling dangerous drugs. He also got eight-to-ten for arson—everything running wild, without pardon or parole.

I left there heading North. After fourteen years I returned to that little small town called Hayti, Missouri.

I went out to the cemetery, and while I was standing there, with my mind going over the past, I reached into my pocket and took out my handkerchief to wipe the cold tears from my face. Suddenly I could feel somebody close by staring at me. I slowly turned around, wiping away the tears. When I got my eyes clear enough to see, I found it was Ronney. He had an armful of roses.

He said, "I just stopped by as always to drop Ruby and the girls a little gift." He went on to say, "Chief Banks saw you drive through town a little while ago and he called me. So here I am. How's it going, Tommie?"

I said, "Well, I'm doing OK. I was just standing here turning back the years."

Ronney said, "I know. Here, I think they would like for you to pass out the gifts this time."

I took the roses from Ronney and walked back and placed one on each one of the graves, even Mr. Morgan's.

Ronney said, "Are you coming over to the house? Clara and the kids would love to see you. You wouldn't know them, Tommie."

I dropped my head and said, "No, I don't think I better, Ronney. Maybe next year."

He said, "Well, I understand, Tommie."

I said, "Do me a favor and don't tell them I was here."

He said, "Sure, Tommie."

I walked over and gave him a bear hug.

I said, "Well, I better be drifting on."

He said, "Where you heading, Tommie?"

I said, "I don't exactly know, Ronney. Maybe some day I'll find a place and settle down."

He said, "You need any money? I got a few bucks to spare."

I said, "No, I am okay for bread. I been taking care of that end pretty good."

He said, "When will you be coming back?"

I said, "Soon. Soon." I took my fist and gave him a tap on the shoulder and said, "Ciao, pal."

He said, "Ciao."

I got in my car and brought it to life. After I had driven about a block or two I looked in the rearview mirror. I could see Ronney standing with his hands in his coat pocket. Just before I turned on the main highway, I hit the horn. Ronney looked up and waved.

Somehow I felt good, but I knew I had to leave that little town that I had loved so well all my life. Even though there will be many Christmases to come for the little town and all its good people. As for me, I knew for the little town called Hayti, Missouri, and time to come, I had spent my *last Christmas*.